Simply
Smocking

Simply
Smocking

Jenny Bradford

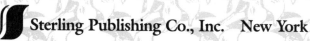
Sterling Publishing Co., Inc.   New York

Library of Congress Cataloging-in-Publication Data

Bradford, Jenny.
    Simply smocking / by Jenny Bradford.
        p.   cm.
    ''First published in Australia in two volumes, Simply smocking in
1988 and Simply smocking 2 in 1989''—T.p. verso.
    Includes index.
    1. Smocking.   I. Title.
TT840.S66B73   1990   90-38648
746.44—dc20   CIP

10 9 8 7 6 5 4 3 2 1

© 1990 by Jenny Bradford
Published by Sterling Publishing Company, Inc.
387 Park Avenue South, New York, N.Y. 10016
Originally published in two volumes, *Simply Smocking* in 1988
and *Simply Smocking 2* in 1989, by Greenhouse Publications Pty Ltd
Distributed in Canada by Sterling Publishing
% Canadian Manda Group, P.O. Box 920, Station U
Toronto, Ontario, Canada M8Z 5P9
Manufactured in the United States of America
All rights reserved

Sterling ISBN 0-8069-7396-X Paper

❧ ACKNOWLEDGMENTS ❧

I hope that every friend, student, and acquaintance who has ever been involved in smocking with me will gain satisfaction from knowing that each of them has played a part in helping me acquire the knowledge and expertise needed to write this book.

Grateful thanks to Jan Kerton of Windflower Smocking, Melbourne, Australia for allowing me to publish her design for the ring pillow and horseshoe and for providing the exquisitely made samples for photography.

Special thanks to Wendy Corke, Lois Kinsman, Neryl Richards, Jenny Salmond and Margaret Wilson for helping me to check pattern sizing, design plates and assist with the samples for photography.

Finally to my husband, Don, and my son Terry for their assistance in numerous ways, including proofreading and drawing the patterns and diagrams, and most of all their continual support.

❧ CONTENTS ❧

Color section follows page 32

❦ INTRODUCTION ❦

The current increase in popularity of smocking is due mainly, I am sure, to the increased availability of pleating machines. Although not new, pleating machines having been available in their present form for over thirty years, their recent wide distribution by some of the main sewing machine companies has brought them to the attention of many more people. Designed to eliminate the tedious process of hand-pleating the fabric to make it ready for smocking, the pleater has enabled us to devote more time to the beautiful and more interesting form of embroidery known as smocking.

With preparation cut to a minimum, the actual time spent in smocking is no greater than for other forms of embroidery, and in some cases, far less.

In addition to the pleating machines now sold through many of the sewing machine company outlets, there are an increasing number of shops and private individuals who will pleat fabric for a very small charge. This service is also available through many embroidery groups, technical colleges and schools. Transfer smocking dots, however, are still available from needlecraft supply shops for those who still wish to use them.

Small projects, such as many detailed in this book, make excellent practice pieces for the beginner. They provide experience in a wide variety of stitches and, equally essential, experience in construction techniques.

The book contains a wide variety of practical ideas for every level of ability. The projects, for example, using counterchange smocking can be completed without pleating the fabric before smocking and they are very economical and easy to work.

Full instructions including patterns, smocking designs, and assembly details, together with advice on the degree of difficulty are given for each project.

MATERIALS

Fabric

Just because you are working a small project and perhaps using it as a practice piece, it does not mean that fabric of any quality can be used. The choice of inappropriate fabric for any smocking project can cause problems.

Frequently, because of the small amount of fabric required, the difference in cost between using top-quality fabric and using inferior and generally more difficult-to-handle fabric is negligible.

Fabric, chosen for the projects in this book, include ribbon, lace edging, voile, silk organza, and fine cotton or cotton blends. They have been selected to make preparation and construction as quick and easy as possible, as well as for their appearance and durability.

I do not suggest that there are no alternatives to the specified fabric; however, if you wish to experiment, be prepared to adjust the designs and techniques accordingly. For example, when substituting heavier fabric for a lighter one, you may not need as large a pleating allowance; with a finer fabric you will need more.

Smocking on a heavier fabric than that recommended may also create problems in construction because of the extra bulk in the seams. In short, the inexperienced smocker is usually better off initially making up the project exactly as recommended and experimenting later when one knows what one is aiming at.

REQUIREMENTS

How much fabric do I need to allow for smocking? This is one of the most frequently asked questions. Unfortunately there is no exact answer. Many factors have a bearing on this and if you understand these you will be able to make small adjustments to any basic pattern to give the desired results.

Weight of Fabric

Very few smocking patterns warn users that the weight of the fabric and the type of smocking design used have a direct bearing on how much the finished piece of work will stretch.

The generally accepted average is to allow three times the width of the finished piece. This estimate is excellent, provided that the fabric to be used is a cotton or poly-cotton of average lawn/poplin weight. A finer fabric will pleat up tighter and therefore a three to four times the width allowance is better, a wool challis or fine corduroy will not pull up as much and two and a half to three times will usually be sufficient.

Smocking designs are given for the projects. Several of these require variation from the general rule, so be sure to adjust the fabric allowance for pleating if you work the article using a different design.

Smocking Design

The second factor to influence the finished size is the type of design chosen for the smocking. Certain stitches, such as Van Dyke and honeycomb take up less fabric than regular smocking stitches. Two and a half times the finished width is sufficient, which makes these stitches ideally suited to projects where less fullness is desirable. Note that this only applies if these stitches are used for the complete design and not if they are mixed in with other stitches.

Stacking designs generally take up more fabric, (three and half to four times the finished width), as there is very little stretch allowed for in the finished piece; which makes this type of design more suitable for insertion panels.

Stretch of Pleats

A third factor that has a direct bearing on the finished width of a panel is how far you personally like to spread the pleats after smocking. Many smockers prefer to see the pleats set relatively close with as little distortion to the design as possible. Having to stretch the pleats too much can cause the fabric to bubble between the stitching, detracting from the geometric appearance of the design.

Embroidery Technique

Finally the tension of the embroidery thread and the depth at which each pleat is picked up both have a slight effect on the elasticity of your work. Inconsistency in these areas will produce uneven work.

Awareness and understanding of these factors should enable most smockers to make the necessary calculations to successfully substitute smocked panels for gathers or pleats in many standard commercial patterns.

It also enables the double checking of a pattern designed for smocking to suit your personal requirements and ensures satisfactory results every time.

Threads

There are many types of embroidery threads suitable for smocking, the most important consideration is that the threads chosen complement the fabric and have the durability necessary for the project.

Stranded cotton threads are the most popular, they are easy to use, available in a large range of colors, they wash and wear well, and they are readily available. The number of strands used can vary from two to four depending on the weight of the fabric and the appearance desired.

Marlitt thread is a four-strand viscose thread and has a beautiful sheen which catches the light and makes the smocking stand out. It is particularly effective when the thread is similar in color to the material being worked. Two strands are usually sufficient but it is not as easy to use as stranded cotton as the strands have a tendency to separate and slip. The color range is good, it washes and wears well and its distribution is becoming fairly widespread.

Other threads that can be successfully used include Cotton Perle (numbers 8 or 12), pure silk, and for projects of a more experimental nature, metallic threads, wools and ribbons should not be ignored.

NEEDLES.

Use a crewel needle. Size seven or eight works well for two or three strands of thread.

TECHNIQUES

Before You Start

Always strip the thread to give the best thread coverage to the stitches. Pull the strands one at a time from the cut length and smooth them back together before threading the needle. (Hold stranded cotton lightly between the thumb and forefinger of the left hand and pull each strand *vertically* away from the main thread. The threads will not twist and tangle as they do when pulled sideways).

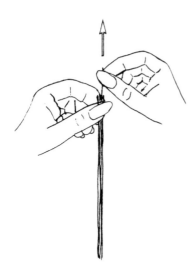

Points to Remember

- Each stitch links two pleats together, but as a general rule the needle picks up only one pleat per stitch.

- Most stitches are worked from left to right. (If you are left-handed work from right to left, and turn the diagrams upside down.)

- Unless specifically directed to the contrary, *never* slope the needle. Always pick up pleats with the needle held at right angles to the pleat and parallel to the pleating threads.

- Where the pattern moves up or down between the pleating threads, follow the golden rule: Thread below the needle if the stitch is going up the work; thread above the needle if the stitch is coming down.

- "Full space" refers to the space between two adjacent pleating threads. So a "half space" is the distance from one pleating thread to a point halfway to the next pleating thread.

- Watch your pattern and count the pleats carefully; mistakes have a way of compounding as the work progresses. There is really no alternative but to go back and correct them.

- Designs should be centered and each row must start and finish at the same point of the pattern.

- To center a design, commence in the center of the work with a zigzag row that establishes the major design reference for the pattern. First work what would normally be the second half of the row, from the center out to the edge. Return to the center, turn the work upside down, and work the other half of the row from the center out to the other edge. Once complete, all other rows can be worked from the left.

- All smocking should be blocked to size before mounting. Remove pleating threads, pin out the smocked piece right side up to the required measurement (adjusting pleats so that they are evenly spaced). Steam the smocking by holding a steam iron close to, *but not touching* the pleats. If the smocked piece does not retain the correct shape when the pins are removed repeat the steaming process.

- Aim for consistency when picking up pleats. The depth of each stitch should be a half to two-thirds of the total depth of the pleat. On machine-pleated fabric, this means almost to the pleating thread.
- To establish the right side of reversible machine-pleated fabric, spread the pleats to expose pleating threads on one corner of the fabric. The length of the pleating thread stitches will be longer on one side of the fabric than the other; this is the wrong side of the fabric. Remember, *long is wrong*.

Pleats

How tightly should the pleats be pulled up and tied off ready for smocking? This is one of the most frequently asked questions. The majority of articles written on this subject give a measurement of anything from 1–4" (2½–10cm) less than the required finished width. This is not necessarily so as it usually results in the pleats being spread too far apart for even stitching. Provided the necessary fabric allowance has been calculated and, having taken into consideration the points already made, there will be sufficient elasticity in the work to fit the pattern. As previously stated, a full width of lightweight fabric such as voile compacts much more than a heavier fabric, such as Vyella, so it is important to adjust the pleats by appearance rather than measurement.

The only consideration then, when tying off the pleats, should be to adjust them to give the best possible results by allowing for ease and evenness of stitching.

Knot the pleating threads together in pairs down one edge of the panel. Keeping this edge straight, gently pull the threads from the other end until all the knots are against the edge.

Hold the knotted edge firmly under the left hand and gently spread the pleats by lightly running the fingers across the fabric. Move up and down the length of the pleated area evenly, maintaining the shape as far as possible. Be careful not to dig your nails into the pleats as this causes uneven spreading. Slight unevenness can be corrected by tightening the threads from the untied edge.

Keep the pleats in straight vertical formation, with just sufficient room to slide the needle between them and permit the pleat you are working on to be moved with the needle to see the pleating threads easily. A further check can be made by holding the pleating sideways over the hand; as the pleats roll over the index finger the pleating threads should be just visible on either side of the uppermost pleat.

Carefully knot the same pairs of threads against the other edge of the fabric to maintain this setting.

HELPFUL HINTS

- Allow an extra pleating thread at the top (and, if working a straight design or panel, at the bottom) for the following reasons:

  It makes the top, and, where necessary, the bottom row of smocking much easier to work and keep even.

  The top thread and, where applicable, the bottom thread, is used to adjust the work for blocking and as a mounting guide when assembling the item. It should be long and left untied during smocking and remain in the work until construction of the project is completed. It is a good idea to *use contrasting threads* for these rows as a reminder.
- To center the pleating machine threads on a narrow strip of fabric (e.g. on a project such as the coat hanger), fold the fabric in half, iron a crease down the center of the strip, unfold, roll carefully and pleat using the crease as a center-line guide.
- Very soft fine fabrics such as voile pleat more crisply if spray starch is used on the pleating area before pleating.

- Closely woven fabrics, such as Liberty cottons, pleat more easily if washed, using fabric softener before pleating.
- Bubbly and/or crossover pleats are usually the result of using crease-resistant fabric or the pleating being off-grain. Avoid spreading the pleats out as they are moved off the pleater needles, ease them off carefully in a block.

Keep the pleats as tight as possible and push the valleys down into position with a blunt needle. The pleats sometimes align themselves correctly if tension is exerted at the top and bottom of the pleats after removing the fabric from the pleater. Once they are correctly positioned, keep the pleats tight and steam thoroughly before adjusting the tension for smocking.

- Take care of your pleater and clean it regularly, paying particular attention to the ends of *all* the brass rollers.
- Take care of your needles; use only the required number in the machine for the project. Always remove and discard bent needles; they will not pick up the fabric accurately and often cause other needles to break.
- For straight panels and bishop designs, put in the required number of needles counting from the *left*-hand side of the machine. Feed the fabric through with the top of the panel at the *right*-hand side of these needles. All excess fabric will be left *outside* the left hand side of the machine.

Note. When finishing pleats with binding cut from lightweight fabric, cut the binding wide enough to use it double. Match the raw edges and press. Attach to the required edge, matching all raw edges. Trim seam if required and fold the binding over and hem along the folded edge by hand. Take care to cut the binding to the correct width in the first place, as there is no adjustment allowed when using this method after the first machine seam has been made.

Smocking

GENERAL

- *Always* strip the thread as it helps to give maximum thread coverage and makes the embroidery stand out. (This applies to all embroidery in which you use stranded threads.)
- Keep the tension even, spacing accurate, and the stitches worked to an even depth across the pleats.

Many smockers pull the stitches too tightly, fearing that the work will be too slack once the pleating threads are removed. This only causes distortion of the pleats, the thread and the pleat intertwine, resulting in poor definition of the stitches and the pattern. The stitches should be worked so that they sit evenly and smoothly around the pleats giving a clear pattern definition that dominates the fabric. This is achieved by smoothing the thread into position rather than tugging it and picking up each pleat at the correct depth.

- Uneven diamonds. When working diamond patterns, using any stitch, remember that the thread lies above or below the needle pick-up point on a cable stitch and allowance must be made for this. Otherwise the top or bottom level cable will encroach on the other half of the space. The pleating thread or an imaginary halfway line should lie directly between the adjacent cables. To achieve this the needle pick-up point for the top- and bottom-level stitches must be at least a needle width away from this line.
- Uneven spacing of stitches is usually a result of lining each stitch up with the previous stitches instead of making sure each stitch position is judged individually in relation to the pleating threads. You need to move each pleat as you work to expose the pleating threads on either

side. Standing the pleat up in this way also enables it to be picked up on the needle evenly, at a constant depth on *both* sides of the pleat and without any danger of catching in either of the adjacent pleats.

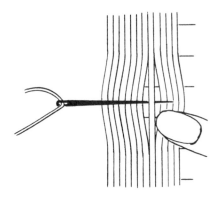

- Avoid unsightly knots on the back of the work. There are several ways of dealing with this problem which can be particularly annoying on very fine sheer fabrics.
- By working from the center of the row out, an extra-long thread may be used. Start in the center of the design, leaving half of the long thread hanging at the back of the work. Complete the row from the center to the right-hand side. Return to the center, rethread the needle, turn the work upside down, and complete the other half of the row. This is the normal method used for centering a design but the whole design may be worked in this manner.
- Highlighting work with flowerettes can leave many ends. Many flowerettes can be worked in vertical lines. If the thread used is not so strong a color as to show through the base fabric, it can be carried vertically down the work from one flower to the next.

  If working across a row, backsmock the thread from one flower to the next, taking care that the stitches do not show through on the front of the work.

- Side knots can often be hidden in a side seam; if not, the following method may prove satisfactory, particularly when the threads used are very fine. Commence smocking in the usual way, but leave the end of the thread hanging and long enough to rethread a needle later. On reaching the end of the row, take the thread to the back of the work through the valley. Satin stitch over this pleat and down or up to the next pleating thread then pass the needle back through the satin stitching carefully and clip off. Rethread the needle at the start of the row and repeat. If the end pleats on the work are stitched down their full length in this way, keeping the stitches neat and tight, the stitching is not visible from the front of the work and it results in a very neat finish on the reverse side.

BACKSMOCKING

Backsmocking is used on the back of the work where there is insufficient smocking on the front to hold the pleats in place once the pleating threads have been removed. On most fabrics there is a risk that the pleats will puff out if the space between the stitches of the design is greater than the distance between two pleating threads.

Work in thread, matching the fabric; two strands of embroidery thread are sufficient. It is important to stitch to no more than one-quarter of the depth of the pleats so that the stitching does not show on the right side of the work. Cable or trellis designs are the usual choice for this process.

Advanced smockers may enjoy experimenting with other stitches which manipulate the pleats to give lovely textured surfaces on the right side of the work.

A row of cable worked behind a pleating thread which is to be used as a mounting guide will hold the pleats in place and prevent distortion during the construction process.

STACKING DESIGNS

Stacking is the term given to picture-smocking. Rows of cables form the main part of the design, worked so that they completely cover the fabric but do not overlap each other.

Successful stacking depends on following the chart accurately, even tension, good thread coverage and plenty of practice. Complete each row of the motif in sequence by working across the design and turning the work after each row. Use a separate needle for each block of color. Leave these needles at the back of the work as required for subsequent rows.

Stacking means that the top-level cables of one row are directly in line with the bottom-level cables of the adjacent row.

Alternating cables means that each row is an exact copy or shadow of the stitches in the adjacent row.

All stacking designs require backsmocking.

The terms picture-smocking and stacking can also be applied to smocking where a design is built up on top of the pleats, using surface embroidery, which is not necessarily composed of smocking stitches.

Both types of work require the fabric to be adequately backsmocked before working the embroidery. Excessive distortion will spoil the look of the design, therefore it is essential that sufficient fabric allowance is made (approximately three and a half to four times the finished width).

I recommend the following method to advanced smockers as one that will enable you to make up your own patterns and designs:

- Prepare the panel and *tie* the pleating threads carefully but *do not cut them short as you will need to loosen the threads later* without removing them from the fabric.
- Work any rows of regular smocking on the front of the fabric, for example any borders.
- Backsmock the *whole* area reserved for stacking or other embroidery.
- Untie the pleating threads and stretch the fabric to finished size, block and steam.

- Retie the threads carefully removing all slackness but maintaining the blocked size of the panel. It is essential to leave the pleating threads in the fabric to act as guidelines for the placement of the design.
- Work the required stacking design, taking care that the threads lie evenly and smoothly. If you prefer, a design can be drawn onto the pleats with a marker pen and filled in with a variety of stitches.
- Floral embroidery looks better if worked in this way as the stitches are not distorted by the blocking process and can be worked to a more pleasing shape.

Ribbon Threading

Very simple smocking designs can be enhanced by the addition of ribbon threaded through the stitches in geometric patterns (Christmas decorations and jewelry roll).

Half- or full-space chevron or Van Dyke stitches are the ones to use as they allow room for the ribbon to pass under the stitching.

The most commonly used ribbon is double-sided satin ribbon in two or three millimeter widths, which is threaded under the stitching with a tapestry needle.

Always block the work to size *before* threading the ribbon to avoid readjusting the ribbon.

Push the needle under a few stitches at a time, pushing the eye down into the pleats as the needle is pulled through. Remove any unwanted twists from the ribbon as you work.

When folding the ribbon to form a zigzag design take the ribbon *over* the stitch immediately following the change of direction fold and make sure you fold the ribbon in the same direction each time.

COUNTERCHANGE SMOCKING

Originally a term used for smocking worked on even check or striped fabrics, thus dispensing with the necessity to pleat the fabric before embroidering it.

This type of smocking requires you to pick up the checks or stripes in perfect geometric formation so as to create a definite color pattern. Pleating is of course necessary when using fabrics without an appropriate design.

Less fabric is used in counterchange smocking as the pleats are pulled out to the full extent of the stretch of the finished piece. This removes all elasticity from the work. The use of less fabric, coupled with the fact that generally fewer rows of embroidery are required than for other smocking designs, means that counterchange smocking is quick, easy and economical.

Stitches which can be used to achieve this type of smocking are limited to cable, Van Dyke and surface honeycomb.

It is easy to make up your own sequence of rows remembering that the basic rules for the design to work are:

- All bottom level stitches on one row must line up with the top level stitches on the row below.
- Every row is worked straight across the fabric without any upward or downward variations.
- Take care not to leave a gap of more than a centimeter between the bottom of one row and the top of the next.

When working on check fabrics pick up alternate checks carefully, picking up the whole check each time and using the line of the checks as a guide.

Striped fabrics are worked in the same way, except that there is no horizontal line to use as a guide. In some cases it may be possible to follow the line of a thread across the fabric, alternatively rule lines across the fabric using a fabric-marking pen at the required intervals.

Any check or striped fabric used in this type of work must be even and symmetrical. *Uneven stripes or checks such as tartan are not suitable for this type of work.*

Fabric allowance may vary slightly according to the width of the stripes or checks being picked up, but in general two to two and a quarter times the finished width is sufficient. Because of the need to stretch the fabric fully to make the pleats sit correctly, allow a little more fabric than might be necessary and leave the ends of each row unfinished so that one or two stitches may be added or removed as required.

Because this type of smocking is stretched very firmly, it is important not to use too fine a thread and to keep in mind that closely matched threads may become almost invisible. A stronger contrast than might normally be used may give a better effect.

This type of smocking has a wide variety of applications apart from the projects detailed in this book. It can be particularly useful where less fullness in a garment may be desirable.

Note: The pleats have been drawn wide apart in the accompanying diagrams in order to clarify the stitch formation. Shaded areas denote valleys and white areas the pleats. The direction of the curve shown on the stitches denotes whether the thread is above or below the needle as the stitch is made.

FINISHING

Blocking: Always block the smocked area as directed. Correct blocking should eliminate the puckering across a yoke often seen on finished work. This is caused by the smocking springing back after being stretched to fit the yoke piece for assembly.

RETAINING ELASTICITY

Continual overstretching of smocking can result in a sloppy fit or broken stitching. Lining the smocked panel will correct this but in some instances this detracts from the snug comfortable fit of the garment.

Backsmocking over a piece of elastic cut to the required size is an excellent way of dealing with this problem, particularly where cuffs, skirt waistbands and sundresses are concerned.

FASTENINGS

Buttonholes do not work well in smocked areas; so try working a button loop instead. Using double thread in the needle make a loop large enough to fit over the button, work two more loops to give six strands of cotton in all. Cover this loop tightly with buttonhole stitch.

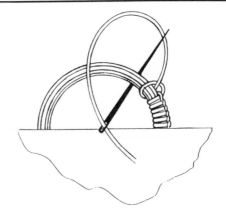

STITCHES

Starting and Finishing A Thread

Starting

Tie a knot in the end of the thread and bring the needle up between the third and fourth pleat from the edge of the fabric. (By leaving two pleats at the *start* and *finish* of the work the seam allowances will remain flat and neat construction will be easier.) Pass the needle to the left through the third pleat (A). Work the first stitch of the design by moving directly across to the fourth pleat (B).

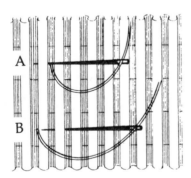

To start a new thread in the middle of a row come up from the back *between* the last two pleats to be stitched together and proceed with the next step of the pattern.

Finishing

Whenever possible, finish with a cable stitch. Complete the stitch and then pass the needle to the back of the work through the valley between the two pleats that are held together by that stitch (C). On the back of the work take a small surface stitch through this pleat and loop the needle through the thread to form a tiny knot (D). This process may be repeated if desired—just to make sure it is secure.

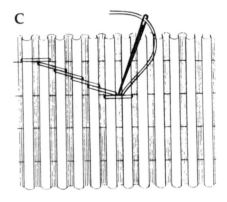

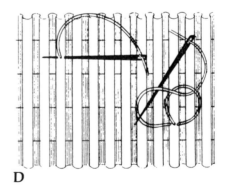

Cable Stitch

Cable stitch is the easiest and most basic of all smocking stitches. It is worked in a straight line across the design and it is invariably worked so that it covers the pleating thread. Position your needle on the left of the third pleat as previously described, lay the thread towards the top of the work and pick up the next pleat, keeping the needle at right angles to the pleat. Gently pull the thread down vertically to tighten the stitch. Leave the thread below the needle while picking up the next pleat (A). Tighten this stitch by gently pulling the thread towards the top of the fabric in line with the pleats.

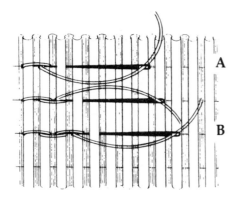

Continue across the row, alternating the thread above and below the needle (B).

Outline and Stem Stitch

Outline stitch—Stitch as before but keep the thread above the needle for every stitch (A).
Stem stitch—Stitch as before but keep the thread below the needle for every stitch (B).

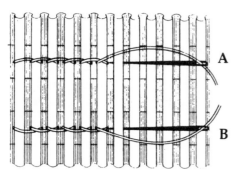

To keep these rows of stitching perfectly straight take care to insert the needle through the pleat in exactly the same place relative to the gathering thread.

Chevron Stitch
(Sometimes referred to as baby wave)
Chevron stitch may be worked over half or full spaces or any combination of these. Commence as before working a bottom level cable over pleats three and four. With the thread below the needle pick up pleat five halfway between the two pleating threads. With the thread above the needle work a level stitch (the top level cable) at this midway point. With the thread above the needle pick up pleat seven in line with the pleating thread.

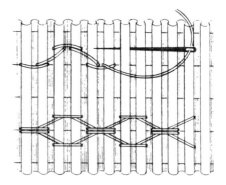

Continue across the row. A second row of chevron worked in exactly the same way under this row is called shadowing. A second row opposing this first row, as a mirror image, creates diamonds.

Trellis Stitch
(Often referred to as wave)
Trellis stitch has infinite variety. It may be worked over half or full spaces in numerous combinations to form waves, hearts and diamonds. The number of stitches and the distance over which they are worked determines the pattern. For example, the diagram opposite depicts a four step, full space

trellis. That is, there are four steps *between* the top and bottom level stitches. Beneath it is a two-step, half-space trellis with a second row worked as a mirror image to form diamonds. Both these waves are worked by picking up each successive pleat at quarter-space intervals.

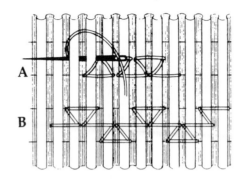

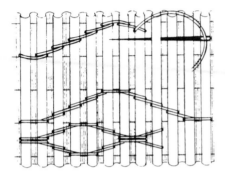

Four-step trellis or wave. Work a bottom level cable, with the thread below the needle. Pick up the next three pleats in turn at the quarter, half and three-quarter space intervals. The fourth step in the trellis is completed as the first pleat of the top level cable is picked up on the pleating thread line. With the thread above the needle complete the top level cable and work four steps down to complete the trellis.

Van Dyke Stitch

Van Dyke stitch is one of the few stitches that is an exception to most of the rules of smocking. As previously stated, less fullness is required as this stitch is shown off to best advantage when stretched right out for finishing.

It is worked from right to left and two pleats are picked up on the needle at once. The stitches can be worked over half or full spacing straight across the row. The diagram shows a row of half-space Van Dyke (A). Alternatively, the stitches

can step down and up to form a zigzag. Row B shows half-space Van Dyke stitches over one full space. The number of steps up and down and the number of spaces involved can be varied to give a variety of zigzag effects.

To work Van Dyke stitch as shown:
- Start on the right-hand side of the work and bring the needle up through the valley between the third and fourth pleat from the edge.
- Take this needle to the left through pleat number four (this is identical to the starting process used on the left-hand side of the work).
- Backstitch pleats three and four together with the thread below the needle.
- Keeping the thread below the needle, move up half a space and pick up pleats four and five on the needle.
- Pull the needle through and then backstitch these two pleats together bringing the needle out below the thread.
- With the thread above the needle move down a half-space and pick up pleats five and six in the same way.

To work a zigzag wave (B) continue stepping down in quarter, half- or full-space steps until the full depth of the wave is achieved before commencing to move up the work again. Remember to keep thread above the needle on all downward stitches and below the needle on all upward stitches.

DECORATIVE HIGHLIGHTS

Double Flowerette

Flowerettes are worked as decorative highlights, often in the center of diamonds. They are worked over four pleats and with the addition of tiny leaves make very pretty flowers. They are interchangeable with grub roses in most designs. To work a double flowerette commence with three

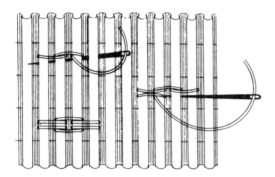

cable stitches—bottom, top, bottom but as the third cable is completed, angle the needle slightly and take it through all four pleats back to the starting position on the left-hand side, a needle width below the first cable. Work a second group of three cables—top, bottom, top, directly under the first three. The needle slope (at the completion of the first set of cables) should allow just enough room for the threads of the adjacent cables to lie flat and not overlap but without any fabric showing through.

Lazy Daisy Stitch

Lazy daisy stitches can be used to form leaves or arranged in groups to form flowers. They will cause less distortion to pleats and be more even if they are worked after the pleating threads have been removed and the work blocked to size.

Bring the needle up through the peak of the pleat, return the needle to the back of the work immediately adjacent to this point leaving a loop of thread on the surface (A). Bring the needle up

through the peak of a pleat the required distance from the original starting point, making sure that the thread loop is around the needle. Adjust the loop to sit neatly on the surface of the pleats and hold it in place by forming a tiny straight stitch over the loop as the needle is returned to the back of the work through the same hole (B).

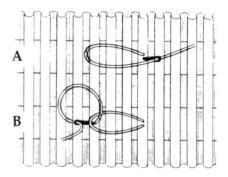

This method gives a more even stitch than the more generally accepted way of sliding the needle through the pleats between step A and B.

Bullion Lazy Daisy

This is an extremely useful stitch for embroidery on smocked pleats. As it sits on top of the pleats, it is much easier to position attractively than ordinary lazy daisy, provided you always return the needle to the back of the work through the peak of the pleats.

A small bullion stitch takes the place of the usual anchor stitch at the point of the petal. To achieve a neat stitch the thread should be kept taut at all times and firmly tightened before anchoring the bullion.

Bring the needle up through the peak of a pleat at A, take it down again at A, or if a wider based petal is required a short distance from A, and out at B. Remember that the bullion part of the stitch will extend beyond this point.

Bring the thread under the point of the needle and wind it around the needle three or four times.

Bring the thread down to the base of the stitch and hold in place gently with the left thumb as you pull the needle through, keeping it close to the fabric and in line with the bullion stitch.

- Turn the needle counterclockwise (left) sliding it under the thread as it reaches six o'clock.
- Bring the needle over the top of the thread and turn it clockwise back to twelve o'clock and pass it back through the peak of the pleat close to, but not through, the original exit hole.

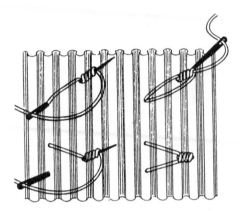

Anchor the bullion by returning the needle through the peak of a pleat at the tip of the bullion. This point will not necessarily be on the same pleat as point B.

Note. If working wide-based petals, as in the waratah, one or two straight stitches may be worked in the center to cover the base fabric.

Colonial Knot

(Also known as candlewicking knot)

This knot has a firmer shape than a French knot and sits well on the pleats.

- Bring the needle up through the peak of a pleat and hold the thread between the thumb and index finger of the left hand about 1½" or 2" away from the exit point.
- Imagining this point as a clock face, hold the needle, pointing to twelve o'clock and pick up the thread from the left side on the point of the needle.

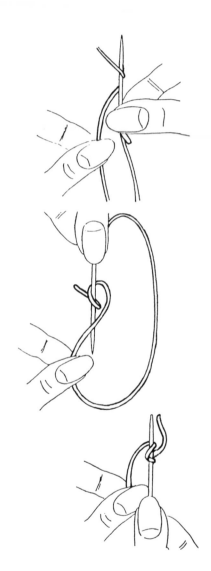

DECORATIVE FRILLS, EDGINGS AND BANDS

To be used on towels, napkin rings and much more.

Counterchange smocking is ideal for working on ribbon or lace edgings, which need no preparation. It can be used as a trim on a wide variety of items.

Bands can be sewn on by hand or machine according to preference or attached with a fabric glue where appropriate, such as the napkin ring pictured.

A few quick ideas are given here but I am sure you will find many more to add to the list. Follow the recommendations given at the beginning of this section for fabric allowance and design and you will be able to make many inexpensive gifts.

TOWELS

The red towel shown in the color section is decorated with a band worked on tartan ribbon. On the other towels pictured a band of 2½" -wide cotton edging has been used. The unfinished edge was turned under and caught into the top pleating thread. Alternatively it can be overlocked in matching or contrasting thread.

NAPKIN RINGS

These are based on cardboard sections cut from a tube of the appropriate size (most fabric shops will be only too happy to give you the tube from a finished fabric roll).

Cut sections from the tube equal to the width of the ribbon and prepare a smocked band to fit snugly around this ring.

To cover the inside of the cardboard ring, cut a bias strip a little less than twice the width of the ring and long enough to fit around it including a seam allowance.

To establish the seam line, stretch it firmly around the outside of the shape and pin the ends together. Remove and sew down the marked seam right sides together. Trim the seam, press open and turn right side out. Fit this tube of fabric inside the ring and fold the top and bottom seam allowance to the outside. Using strong thread, lace the raw edges over the ring, pulling the fabric as tightly as possible. Smooth a little glue around the center of the ring, over the lacing thread and carefully slip the smocking into place.

Try using counterchange smocking to decorate place mats, book covers, tissue boxes, photo frames, belts and bags.

TENSION

As with all embroidery an even stitch tension is essential for the best results. Care should be taken to take every stitch to the same depth into the pleat (one half to two thirds of the total depth for regular smocking and a quarter of the depth for back smocking). Each stitch should be tightened just sufficiently to lay the threads over the pleats smoothly without distorting them in any way. Pulling the thread too tightly around the pleats, at this stage, results in the pleats twisting and obscuring the stitches when the work is blocked to size for mounting.

ASSEMBLING AND
FINISHING TECHNIQUES

Finishing Edges

Finish all frilled edges that will be close to smocked areas before pleating. Alternatively, pleating threads must be left long enough for the pleats to be smoothed out if finishing is to be done later, but always finish before smocking is commenced.

The finish chosen will depend on the type of equipment available and the type of project involved.

One of the most useful ways of finishing the edges of fine fabrics is with a rolled hem; this can be achieved by hand, using a regular sewing machine or with an overlocker.

The quickest method is to use an overlocker and if a contrasting color filler or fluffy thread is used on the overlooper a very attractive decorative edge is created. Follow the manufacturer's instructions for setting up the machine correctly.

Fluffy or filler thread is available in a wide range of colors from haberdashery or sewing machine supply shops.

Fabrics to be finished by hand or sewing machine should be fine and the edges cut not torn. If possible use a very fine sewing thread (number 60 cotton) available from specialist shops handling heirloom and fine sewing supplies.

ROLLING AND WHIPPING BY MACHINE

Set machine-stitch length to just longer than satin stitch and the stitch width set so that the needle catches about ¹⁄₁₆″ (2mm) of fabric and clears the raw edge as it moves from side to side. *Tighten* the tension on the top thread and work with the fabric wrong side up. As you stitch, the fabric will be rolled over to form a very fine hem.

To attach lace to these edges use a normal zigzag stitch setting as fine as is practicable and place the lace and fabric edge to edge right sides up. Zigzag together.

ROLLING AND WHIPPING BY HAND

Use a fine needle. Waxing the thread with beeswax will add strength while working. Place your needle against the right-hand edge of the fabric to be hemmed, damp the thumb and index finger of your left hand and gently roll the edge of the fabric over the needle (A).

Withdraw the needle gently, holding the roll in place with the left thumb and finger. Insert the

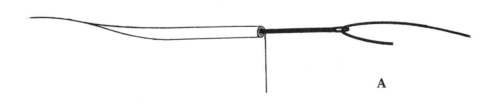

A

Brunch coat with lace collar over a matching nightgown, shown with another nightgown.

A nightgown made with either a cap sleeve or shoestring tie. The coat hanger, lingerie bag and tiny tissue pack are quick and easy to make.

A lovely ring pillow, a horseshoe for good luck and a garter for "some-thing blue." The decorated towels are a practical wedding present. Also pictured is a jewelry roll.

D

Some examples of a wide range of stitches and how they can be used.

Above are some selections for baby: picture smocking in a quilt or wall hanging, bib and bootees for a christening, even a bib for Teddy.
At right is a gown and matching jumpers for both baby and teddy bear.

Christmas decorations and napkin rings shown above are easy to make. Here also is a child's sundress and a dress for her doll, along with a sewing roll.
At left are two smocked collars, one for the girl's dress and one for her teddy bear.

Appliquéd panels can be attached to ready-made garments.

H

Here is one of the pleating machines that are responsible for much of the new interest and enthusiasm of embroiderers for smocking. It cuts the preparation time to a minimum.

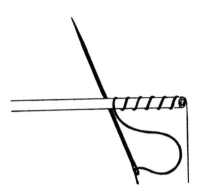

needle under the roll and slide it out through the top at an angle of 45 degrees, catching the roll of fabric only (B). Repeat stitches at about 1/16" intervals (1–2 mm), tightening the thread every few stitches. Continue rolling and stitching along the edge. Tensioning the fabric by anchoring it firmly at the starting point will assist your rolling process, which once having been started with the needle can be continued by using damp fingers only.

To attach lace or entredeux to this edge, hand-whip with tiny stitches.

SEAMS

Where it is necessary to pleat over a seam it is essential to keep the bulk of the seam to a minimum. I do not recommend French seams except possibly on the finest of voiles. Overlocked seams, provided the fine overlocking thread is used, are the least obtrusive seams and they cause fewer problems with the pleater. Overlocking on a regular sewing machine, using normal sewing thread, is not as successful and in this case an open seam (trimmed back in the area to be pleated) is the most satisfactory. If neatening is required this may be done by hand after the smocking is completed.

BIAS BINDING

When using lightweight fabrics cut twice the required width and use the bias binding folded double. Iron, matching cut edges and stitch in place, matching all the raw edges. Turn and hem along fold. This method is neater, easier to sew and the double thickness of fabric covers the bulk of the pleats more satisfactorily.

Be sure to calculate the width required carefully as there is no adjustment once the band is stitched in place.

FRILLED EDGES

Frilled edges on unlined panels will need stabilizing to prevent excessive stretch. Where any stretch is undesirable ribbon can be used, threaded through the smocking stitches and adjusted to size. A row of chevron backsmocking may be used if the design does not allow for this.

QUILTING

Quilted fabric is used in many of the projects as it provides the necessary firmness to support the smocking.

The choice of readymade quilted fabric can be very limited so I suggest purchasing the quilted fabric and then color-coordinating the rest of the fabric for your project to it.

Quilting your own fabric is not difficult, especially when only small pieces are required.

Full instructions follow in this section.

Quilting by Machine

First check your sewing machine instruction book; it may contain relevant information for your type of machine. Most sewing machine companies supply a quilting guide in their accessory kit. A quilting guide is a long metal prong with a bar at one end; if you have one you will also have a sewing foot with a hole in the back of it into which the long prong will fit. A small screw tightens onto the prong to hold it firm. If you do not have these fittings it may be possible to obtain them from the local agent or supplier of your brand of machine.

The prong guide is adjustable and you set it to give you rows of equally spaced stitching without having to mark the fabric in any way. Once the first row is stitched the bar at the end of the guide is run in line with each successive row as you move across the fabric.

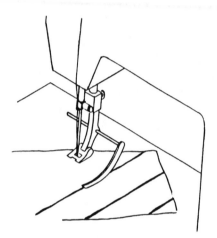

- Never tack the fabrics together as you need to be able to smooth the top fabric as you go to prevent small wrinkles. If necessary pin the fabric and remove the pins as you come to them.
- I find working on the diagonal the easiest way, with the first row being a very short one across the bottom right corner. Any slight discrepancies in a diagonal pattern are not as obvious as those in a pattern that is intended to be parallel to the sides of your work.
- Experiment with your machine quilting. Using a twin needle is very effective and some of the decorative stitch settings can be used to great effect. Serpentine and three-step zigzag are two of the commonly available stitches to try. (Be careful if using a twin needle with a zigzag

setting not to set the zigzag too wide or the needle will swing too far and break on the foot.)

Matching or contrast sewing thread can be used, however the shiny machine embroidery threads now available give a very attractive finish. (Wind a spare bobbin from the main reel to use for the second needle if working with a twin needle.)

- Use a firm batting which will hold its shape and not catch on the feed teeth of the machine. Most stores selling quilted supplies stock this type of batting which is usually approximately 27½" (70cm) wide. Soft fluffy batting used for hand-quilting is not suitable.
- Always quilt a piece slightly larger than the size required and cut your pattern out afterwards. If you do this you will have a neat edge and any slight distortion that might occur in quilting will not be transferred to your project.

Method for Quilting Small Pieces

- Cut a piece of fabric and a piece of batting.
- Pin the pieces together moving across the fabric from the bottom right-hand corner to the top left-hand corner.
- Set up the machine according to the manufacturer's instructions. Work a small test piece to check tension and spacing.
- Stitch across the bottom right-hand corner, starting and finishing 1" (2 to 2.5cm) from the corner.
- Line the stitched row up with the bar on the quilting guide and stitch a second row.
- Repeat across the fabric, smoothing the surface carefully as you stitch.

To Appliqué A Panel

- Smock and block the panel to required size.
- Using grosgrain ribbon, fancy braid or fabric strips cut to size, pin or tack in place around the edges of the panel. These strips can be arranged to form part of the overall design.

- Stitch carefully round the edges that overlap the smocked panel.
- Trim away seam allowance on the smocked panel if required.
- Working with the garment on a flat surface, pin or tack the ribbon carefully along the outer edges. Stitch in place.

Smocked Pockets

- Cut the panel to size, prefinish the top edge with a hem or lace unless the top edge is to be bound.
- Smock and block the panel to size using the lining as a guide.
- Fold in the hem allowance on the top edge of the lining. Match the lining to the pocket, wrong sides together, with the fold along the top row of smocking.

  Machine or tack around the sides and bottom. Hand hem the top edge to the pleats.

  To bind the top edge of a pocket allow extra fabric at the top edge of the lining. Match the top edges of the smocked panel and lining right sides together. Stitch close to the top row of smocking, trim the seam if necessary and fold the lining to the back of the pocket.

  The binding will show on the front of the pocket as it is turned back over the pleats allowing them to remain flat.

- Add strips of fabric or ribbon along the sides and bottom of the pocket and attach as for an appliqué panel.

INSERTED PANELS

Window mounting is the easiest neatest way of inserting a small panel.

- Smock and prepare the panel for mounting.
- Measure the panel carefully for *finished size*.

- Using a fabric marker, mark the finished size carefully on the wrong side of the item into which the panel is to be mounted.
- Cut a facing of lightweight color matched fabric, adding 2″ (5-cm) turnings all around the finished size of the panel.

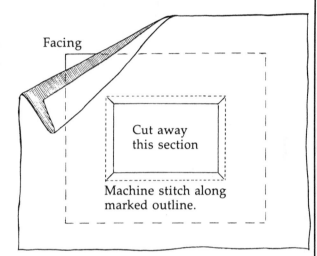

Facing

Cut away this section

Machine stitch along marked outline.

- Place fabrics, right sides together, centering facing over the panel placement area. Machine-stitch around the marked outline on the wrong side.
- Cut out the center of the panel area, leaving a turning of ³⁄₁₆″–³⁄₈″ inside the stitching line. Clip the turning into the corners or around the curves (see diagram). Turn the facing through the hole to the back of the work pressing along the seamline carefully.
- Center the opening over the smocked panel and tack in place carefully. Topstitch through all thicknesses.
- Cover the stitching with lace or braid if desired. Trim and neaten the edges of the smocked panel.

Key to Smocking Diagrams

 Cable

 Half-space Van Dyke

 Half-space Chevron

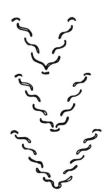 Full-space Chevron

Two-step Half-space Wave

Three-step Full-space Wave

Four-step Full-space Wave

Five-step Full-space Wave

 Backsmocked Cable

 Backsmocked Outline

 Backsmocked Four-step Wave

Double Flowerette with Leaves

 Half-space Stair-step Chevron

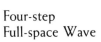 Half-space Chevron with Zigzag Ribbon Threading

 Beads Centered over Adjacent Cables

PATTERNS

Coat Hanger, Lingerie Bag and Tissue Pack

CABLE COAT HANGER

Requirements

Fabric (cotton voile or similar) 5½″ × 35½″ (14 × 90cm)
Batting to pad the coat hanger
Wooden coat hanger
Satin bias for covering the metal hook
Satin ribbon ⅛″ × 43¼″ (3mm wide, 110cm)

Degree of difficulty: Smocking very easy. Construction very easy.

The items as pictured are all made from cotton voile pleated on a pleating machine. Check or stripe fabric can also be used and should be worked according to the instructions given for counter-change smocking.

Smocking

- Finish the long edges of the fabric strip.
- Pleat the fabric, centering 7 pleating rows across the strip.
- Tie off the pleating threads.
- Follow the design from the chart, working across 145 pleats, using 3 strands of DMC cotton or your preferred thread.

A rolled hem edge or lace is used to finish the edges before smocking. If this is done prior to pleating, care must be taken not to distort the edge by over-stretching or pulling too tightly. If preferred, pleat the fabric first, allowing extra long pleating threads so that the strip may be flattened out for edging.

Row 1

Row 2

Row 3

Row 4

Row 5

Row 6

Row 7

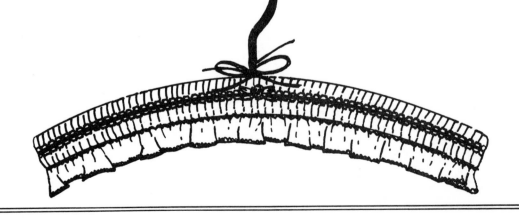

Assembly

- Cover the hook with satin bias binding. Re-press the binding with one raw edge across until it almost touches the other folded edge and press. Fold in half again and stitch carefully with a tiny zigzag stitch very close to the edge, folding in one end as you stitch. Slip over the hook, pull down tightly and trim to expose the screw end.

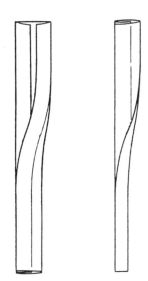

Folded binding for coat hanger.

- Remove all pleating threads.
- Stretch the pleating firmly until the pleats open up evenly. Pin out and steam carefully.
- Thread the satin ribbon through the Van Dyke stitch row.
- Work any bullion roses or lazy daisy flowers required.
- Remove the hook and sew the batting around the wooden coat hanger.
- Sew the short ends of the smocked piece, right sides together, taking care not to pull the ribbon insertion too tight. Turn right side out.
- Taking care not to cut the smocking thread, make a small hole for the hook in the center of Row 5 on the smocked piece.

- Stretch the smocking over the hanger. Locate the screw hole with a needle and line up with the hole in the smocked fabric. Screw in the hook.
- Secure the hook cover with a few stitches around the base of the hook. Trim with ribbon as desired.
- Stab-stitch the lower edge together along Rows 1 and 7 of the smocking, if desired (the cover will sit neatly without this stitching if preferred).

LINGERIE BAG

Requirements

Fabric (cotton voile or similar) 33½" × 13¾" (84 × 35cm)
Satin ribbon ⅛" × 33¾" (3mm wide, 85cm)

Smocking

- Finish the short edges of the fabric.
- Pleat 9 rows across one short end with the top row of pleating 2" (5cm) from the finished edge.
- Working across the center, 45 pleats follow the design from the chart, using 3 strands of DMC cotton or your preferred thread.

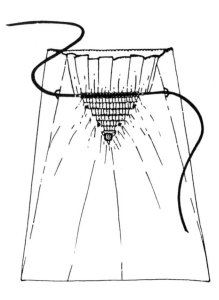

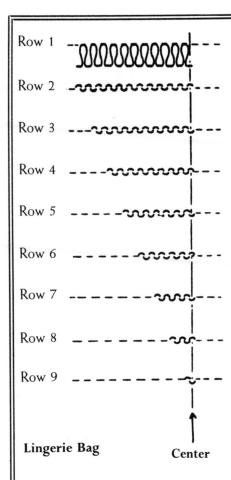

Row 1

Row 2

Row 3

Row 4

Row 5

Row 6

Row 7

Row 8

Row 9

Lingerie Bag   Center

Assembly

- Remove all pleating threads.
- Stretch the pleating firmly until the pleats open up evenly (pin into shape and steam carefully).
- Fold the fabric in half, wrong sides together, carefully matching finished top edges. Sew side seams, using a fine French seam.
- Thread the satin ribbon through the Van Dyke stitch row, leaving a short end (24 cm or 9½″) on the right-hand side of the row.
- Stitch the ribbon firmly in place at each end of the smocking.
- Decorate the smocked panel with further embroidery, such as bullion roses, if desired.
- Work buttonhole loops on the side seams to carry the ribbon ties. In this case the loop can be made to lie flat along the seam.

POCKET TISSUE-PACK COVER

Requirements

Fabric: A 6¼″ × 44″ (16 × 112cm) strip of voile will make three covers (60 pleats required for each cover)

Lining fabric 6″ × 7½″ (15 × 19cm) for each cover

Satin ribbon ⅛″ × 31″ (2 or 3mm wide, 80cm) for each cover

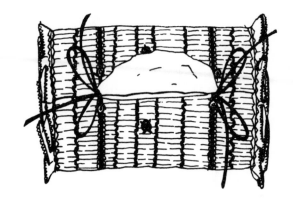

Smocking

- Finish the long edges of the strip, which should then be 6″ (15cm) wide.
- Pleat with 15 rows of pleating threads, centering carefully.
- Allow 2 pleats on either side of each panel for seam allowances. Work the design across 60 pleats according to the chart.

Row 1 --~~~~~~~~--

Row 2 --~~~~~~~--

Row 3 --~~~~~~~--

Row 4 __~SSSSSSSS__--

Row 5 --~~~~~~~~--

Row 6 --~~~~~~~~--

Row 7 --~~~~~~~~--

--~~~~~~~-- ← Center

Row 8 --~~~~~~~--

Pocket Tissue Pack Cover

Assembly

- Remove the pleating threads.
- Stretch the pleating firmly to measure 6″ × 6¾″ (15 × 17cm) plus seam allowance.
- Prepare the lining by turning and pressing the seam allowance (1 cm or ⅜″ wide) on the long edges.
- Center the lining and the smocked panel right sides together and stitch down the short edges against the edges of the smocked panel. Turn right side out.
- Hem the lining along the top and bottom across the back of the pleats.
- Fold the panel in half so that the ends meet at the center front.
- Machine-stitch firmly across the ends between the 2 rows of smocking.
- Thread ribbon through the Van Dyke rows and stitch firmly on each side of the opening. Decorate with bullion rosebuds as desired.
- Insert tissue pack and tie ribbons.

Horseshoe, Ring Pillow and Garter

Degree of difficulty: Horseshoe, smocking easy, construction intermediate; pillow, smocking easy, construction intermediate; Garter, smocking and construction easy.

The lovely gifts of the horseshoe and ring pillow have both been designed and worked by Jan Kerton of Windflower Smocking, Melbourne.

The horseshoe can be either shaped before smocking or smocked first on the straight and fanned into shape.

HORSESHOE

⅜″ (1cm) seam allowance included throughout.

Requirements

Fine cotton 12″ × 45½″ (30 × 115cm)
Fine lace edging 47¼″ (120cm)
Ribbon ⅝″ × 39¼″ (10mm wide, 100cm)
62 small pearls

Pleating and Smocking

- Cut a strip of fabric 3¼″ × 45½″ (8cm wide and 115cm long). Finish one long edge with lace and mark the center on the unfinished edge.
- Pleat with 7 full-space or 12 half-space rows, commencing the firest row ½cm in from the unfinished edge.
- If you wish to shape the horseshoe at this point, cut a template of the horseshoe pattern and pin it to the ironing board. Pin the pleated fabric over the template matching the inner edges and fanning the outer edge evenly to fit the horseshoe. Pin firmly and tie off the pleating threads and smock with given design.

Alternatively, tie-off threads, except for the top and bottom ones, and smock the fabric in a straight strip.

Pearls usually have large enough holes to be threaded as you smock. When positioning a

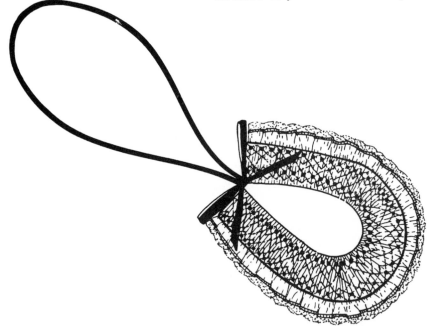

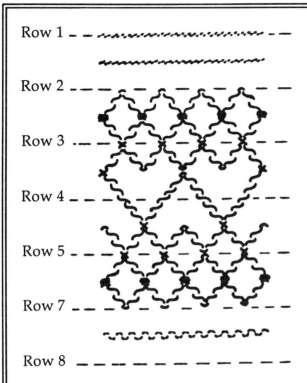

Row 1

Row 2

Row 3

Row 4

Row 5

Row 7

Row 8

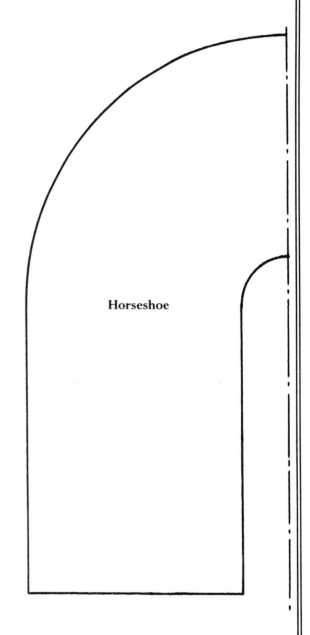

Horseshoe

- Stitch a ribbon loop finished with bows to the ends of the horseshoe so that it hangs correctly and the good luck doesn't run out.

pearl where two cable stitches meet, always add the pearl when working the second cable to ensure that it sits on the surface and is not lost in the valley of the pleats.

Assembly

- Leaving the top and bottom pleating threads in, pin and shape the piece on the template. Steam to set the pleats.
- Cut out the horseshoe shape in fabric. Prefinish the outside edge with lace if desired.
- Place right sides together with the pleated section. Matching inside edges carefully, sew allowing one centimeter seam allowance. Trim the seam and turn right side out.
- Pin outside edges together along the cable holding row. If prefinished, the backing edge is left flat. Alternatively, turn under the edge to match the backsmocking and stitch carefully following the cable stitching line.
- Stuff carefully, shaping as you go. Turn in the seam allowance across the ends and stitch by hand.

RING PILLOW

Finished size 8″ × 6½″ts (20cm × 16cm), excluding the frill. A 1 cm (⅜″) seam allowance included throughout.

Requirements

Fine cotton 45½″ × 23½″ (115cm wide, 60cm)
Lace for edging 68″ (170cm)
200 small pearls
Dacron filling
Ribbon ⅜″ × 39½″ (10mm wide, 100cm)

Pleating and Smocking

Pleat a strip of fabric 9⅛″ × 45½″ (23 × 115cm) with 19 full-space rows.

The smocking design is worked across 140 pleats. Row 10 on the chart is the center row of the design; Rows 11 to 19 are a mirror image of Rows 1 to 9. See notes in beading in instructions for horseshoe.

Assembly

- Cut 2 panels 9⅛″ × 7½″ (23 × 19cm), one for lining the front panel and one for backing the pillow. Cut and piece 8-cm-wide strips to make the frill 66″ (168cm) long. Finish one edge with lace. Double fullness has been allowed for the frill.
- For even distribution of the frill mark it into 4 sections, each twice the length of a side of the cushion panel.
- Gather the frill with 2 rows of machine gathers.
- Sew the ends of the frill together.
- Block and steam the smocked panel to fit the lining panel and tack the 2 wrong sides together.
- Position the gathered frill on the pillow panel, right sides together, matching the raw edges with the 4 section marks at the corners of the pillow.
- Sew the frill into place.
- Position the backing panel right sides together

over the frill and pin or tack in place. Machine through all thicknesses, from the wrong side of the front panel, following the frill stitching line and leaving an opening for turning.
- Turn the pillow right side out, stuff firmly and hem the opening closed.
- Cut ribbon to desired length to make one or two ties to hold the rings in place. Stitch into position.

Ring Pillow

A PRETTY GARTER
FOR THE BRIDE

This is very quick and easy.

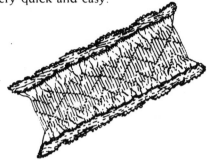

- Pleat the fabric, using shirring elastic for the pleating threads.
- Leave elastic untied, smock with a narrow straight design.
- Adjust the size before joining the seam and finishing off the elastic threads which can be sewn into the seam or knotted together.
- Finish both edges of a narrow strip of fabric 3 times the required finished length.

Child's Sundress or Skirt

Degree of difficulty: Smocking easy, construction easy.
Size 2 upward

Fabric Requirements:

Two pieces full width (115 cm or 45½ in) and cut to the length required. 4-in (10-cm) strips for straps.

This will fit up to a 25½-in (65-cm) chest or waist measurement. Allow extra width for larger sizes. Wash the fabric before cutting.

- Pleat with 7½ rows of pleating. Using a half-space row very close to the top edge will make the frill at the top edge narrow and more comfortable under the arms (particularly on the smaller sizes).
- Smock the given design, dropping off as many pleats as necessary to ensure the correct pattern match on the seam line.
- Remove the pleating threads and trim the seam if necessary.
- In this case, the smocking will remain more elastic and fit more snugly if the work is not blocked. If desired, elastic can be used around the top edge to hold it firm. Backsmock with a row of full-space chevron over a piece of elastic cut to fit the child.
- Close the second side seam entirely or, depending on the size and shape of the child, you may prefer to leave an opening at the upper edge. If this is the case, close with an open seam, hemming the seam allowance back above the opening and attaching buttons and loops for closing.
- Make straps by stitching a 4″ (10-cm) wide strip of fabric down the long edge. Turn right side out. Press and attach to dress or skirt, adjusting to correct length or leave them long to tie on the shoulders.

- Finish hem to the required length.
- Join the fabric down one side seam using the finest seam possible.
- Finish the top edge with a rolled-hem edge or a very fine hem.

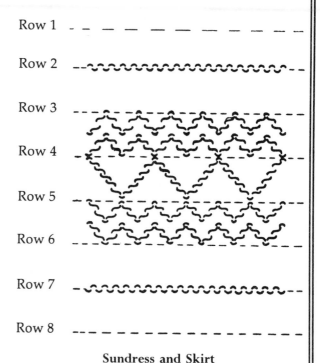

Sundress and Skirt

Dress and Pants for Toys

Degree of difficulty: Smocking very easy, construction very easy.

To fit a doll or teddy bear, measuring approximately 12 in (30cm) around the underarm.

Requirements

Fabric: Dress 35½″ × 5½″ (90 × 14cm) or depth required

Pants: 28½″ × 5½″ (72 × 14cm)

Straps: 3 cm wide strip × approximately 12½″ (32cm) or substitute suitable ribbon

Satin ribbon: 20″ of ⅛″ wide

Smocking

- Finish the top edge of the dress with a decorative edge, with lace or by overlocking.
- Pleat with six rows of half-space pleating.
- Smock the design, dropping as many pleats as necessary to make the pattern match at the center back.
- Remove the pleating threads and join the seam.

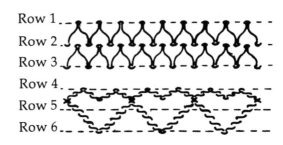

Row 1
Row 2
Row 3
Row 4
Row 5
Row 6

Doll's Dress

- Finish the straps by seaming and turning or by using a decorative edge to match the dress. Try on the dress and pin the straps to fit neatly over the shoulders. Stitch in place.
- Finish the hem to the required length.
- Thread 2mm ribbon through the top row of chevron, commencing at the center front of the dress.

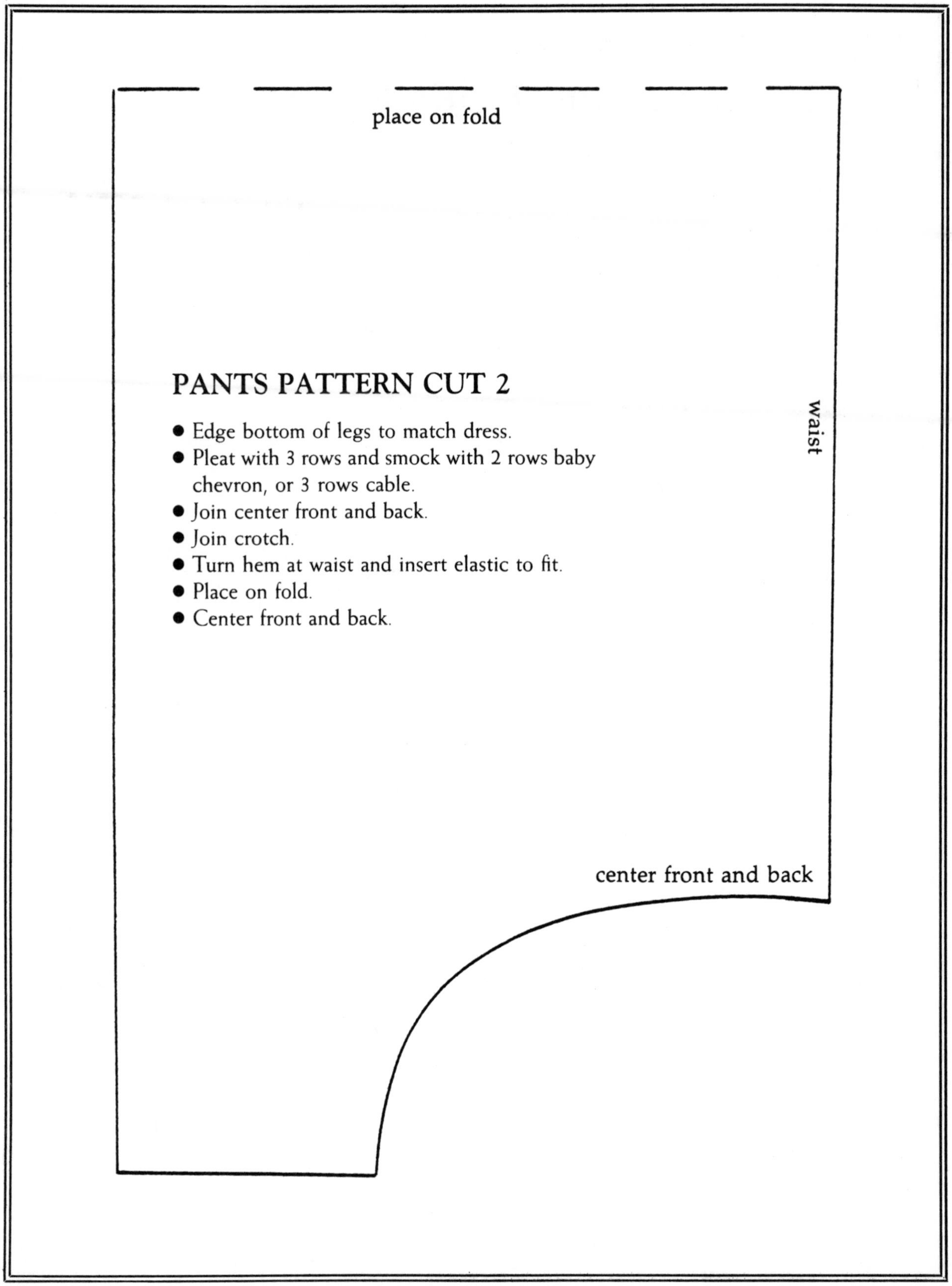

place on fold

waist

PANTS PATTERN CUT 2

- Edge bottom of legs to match dress.
- Pleat with 3 rows and smock with 2 rows baby chevron, or 3 rows cable.
- Join center front and back.
- Join crotch.
- Turn hem at waist and insert elastic to fit.
- Place on fold.
- Center front and back.

center front and back

Nightgown

		A (size 10–12)	B (size 14–16)
Finished length	short	39"	41"
	long	52"	54¾"
Fabric required	(fine voile or cotton/polyester)		
	short	2½ yds	2¾ yds
	long	3½ yds	3¾ yds
	lace	4 yds	4⅛ yds

Degree of difficulty: Smocking easy, construction easy.

This versatile design suits anyone. It is equally attractive, made with the cap sleeve or shoestring ties. Sizes given are for 10 to 12 (A) and 14 to 16 (B) and patterns are given in two lengths.

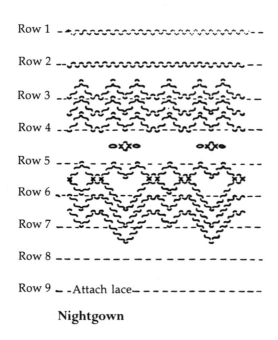

Nightgown

Before commencing please read ALL instructions.

- Cut out the gown according to the diagram, using the sleeve pattern and armhole guides given. *Mark the armhole cutting line on the front panel, but DO NOT CUT along it until the smocking has been completed.*
- Pleat the front panel with 9 rows of pleating threads, cutting the threads long enough to allow the panel to be spread flat after pleating.
- Smooth out the pleats. Attach lace along the line of the ninth pleating thread using a fine zigzag stitch. This ensures that the lace is spaced evenly below the smocking.
- Pull up the pleating threads and tie off all except the top thread. Smock the panel according to the design.

ASSEMBLY

Nightgown with Sleeves

- Remove the pleating threads and cut out the armhole. Block and steam the smocking, pulling up the neck thread to measure 9" (23 cm) for size A and 10" (25 cm) for size B.
- Machine-gather the neck edge of the back panel and pull it up to measure 2¼" (6 cm) longer than the front panel.
- Machine-gather the top edge of the sleeves between notches and finish the lower edge with a narrow hem and lace or trim as desired.
- Pin and sew the sleeves to the front and back, matching the notches on the sleeves to the *top* edges of the front and back.
- Join side seams using a fine French or over-locked seam.
- Bind the armhole from the front neck edge to the back neck edge with a bias strip cut 1" (2.5cm) wide.

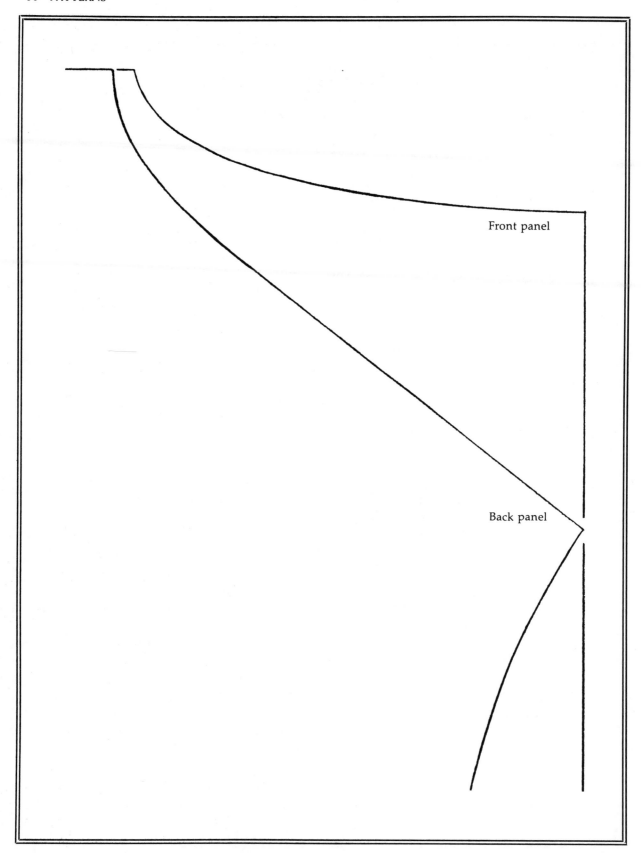

Front panel

Back panel

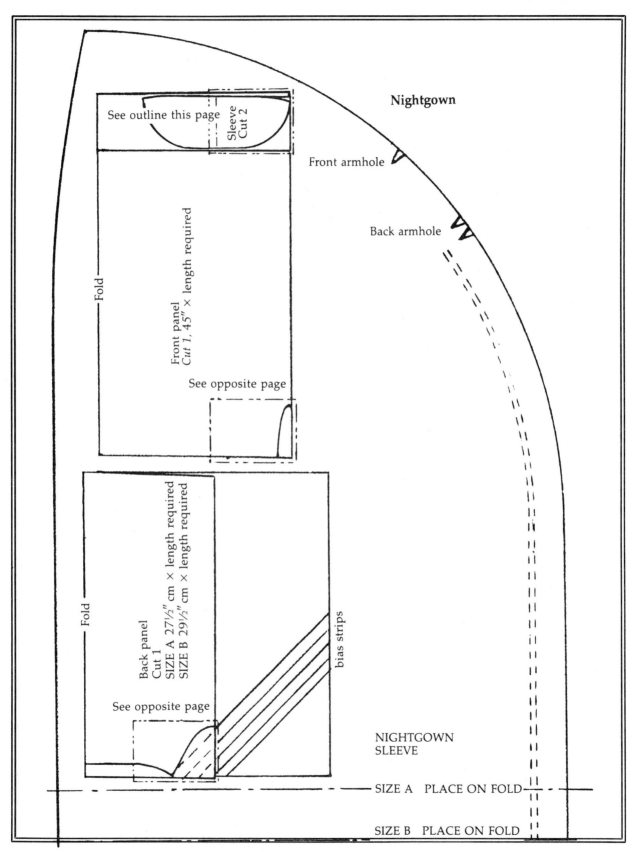

Nightgown

Front armhole

Back armhole

See outline this page

Sleeve
Cut 2

Fold

Front panel
Cut 1, 45" × length required

See opposite page

Fold

Back panel
Cut 1
SIZE A 27½" cm × length required
SIZE B 29½" cm × length required

See opposite page

bias strips

NIGHTGOWN
SLEEVE

SIZE A   PLACE ON FOLD

SIZE B   PLACE ON FOLD

- Pull up the top of the sleeves to measure 10¼" (26cm) (A) and 11" (28cm) (B). If possible, try on the gown to check the neckline and adjust the gathers as necessary. *Adjustment to the gathers across the top of the sleeve will result in increasing or decreasing the size of the armhole.*
- Encase the neck edge with a bias strip cut 1" (2.5cm) wide and the length required; it may be necessary to piece this binding. Satin binding may be used if preferred.
- Finish the gown to the desired length with a narrow hem and lace.

Nightgown with Shoestring Ties

- Prepare front and back panels according to the previous instructions.
- Bind the top edges of the front and back with bias binding.
- Sew side seams.
- Bind the armhole edges, extending binding into ties on the shoulder.
- Finish hem to desired length.

Spectacle Case

Degree of difficulty: Smocking advanced, construction easy.

See the general instructions for picture smocking.
The finished size is 7″ × 3½″ (18 × 9cm). The finished size of this smocked panel is 7″ × 7″ (18 × 18cm).

Requirements

Fabric for outside pleated panel: 25½″ × 8″ (65 × 20cm) and one piece fabric: 15¾″ × 8½″ (40 × 22cm)

Binding strip (straight grain): 15¾″ × 1¼″ (40 × 4.5cm)

Batting: 15″ × 8¾″ (40 × 22cm)

Fastener

Smocking

- Pleat outside panel with 18 rows of pleating threads.
- Secure threads carefully so that they can be loosened later.
- Commencing in the top left-hand corner on the second pleating thread down, work the stair-step chevron design as shown in the chart.
- Backsmock Rows 1 and 18 with cable and the four-step diamond pattern as shown on the chart.
- Prepare the panel as described, blocking and steaming to 7″ × 7″ (18 × 18cm) plus seam allowances (1cm on all sides).

Embroidery

WARATAH. This is partly smocked and can only be worked in this way if the panel is to be mounted sideways.

The cone is smocked with outline and stem stitch worked very close to cover the background fabric completely. Position the center line of the cone directly over a pleating thread.

- Commence stitching at the center point of the base of the cone and work 3 stem stitches.
- Return the needle to the starting point and work 4 stem stitches directly above the previous 3, slanting the fourth stitch towards the pleating thread.
- Turn the work and position 4 outline stitches down the other side of the foundation row.
- Continue building the cone in this way, increasing on each row until 9 stitches are worked on each side.
- Work 2 more rows of 9 stitches on each side to complete the cone.
- Work wide-based bullion lazy daisy petals around the base of the cone. Use straight stitches to fill in the petals.
- The waratah stem is worked in stem stitch in brown.

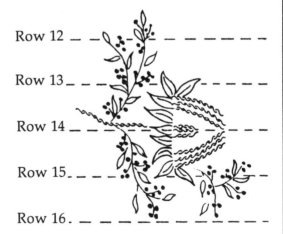

WATTLE. This is worked around the waratah, using colonial knots for the flowers, bullion lazy daisy for leaves and the stems are couched with a single strand of thread.

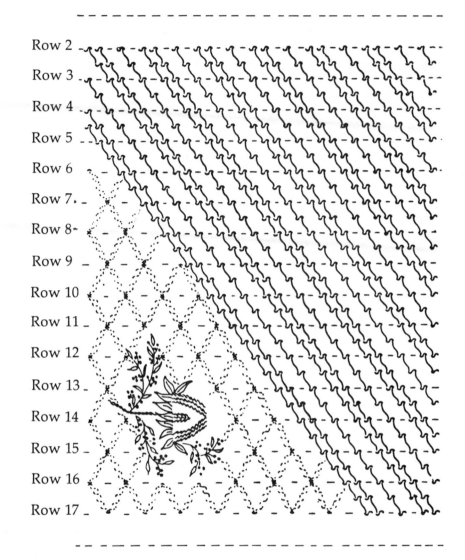

Row 2
Row 3
Row 4
Row 5
Row 6
Row 7
Row 8
Row 9
Row 10
Row 11
Row 12
Row 13
Row 14
Row 15
Row 16
Row 17

Color Key
Original worked in Soie d'Alger — Gold 522, Red 945, Green 1842 and 1843.
Alternatively, D.M.C. — Gold 743, Red 304, Green 522, 524.

Assembly

- Quilt the lining and the batting together. Trim carefully to measure 14″ × 8″ (36 × 20cm).
- Match smocked panel and lining panel right sides together. Stitch carefully across the short ends using a zipper foot to fit snugly against the pleats.

- Turn right sides out and fold carefully along the lower edge of the front flap (the floral embroidery is in the lower right-hand corner).
- Tack or pin the side edges together in line with the cable rows of the smocked panel.
- Machine-stitch and trim seam allowance.
- Form the pocket by folding the quilted section to the inside along the line of the smocking pleats. Stitch in place.
- Bind the side edges with a straight strip of fabric.
- Sew fastener in place.

This pattern can be enlarged to make an envelope style bag.

The white spectacle case pictured on the back cover shows a design worked on the straight rather than the diagonal.

Shaded scallop borders are worked at the top and bottom of the panel in combination with 8 rows of four-step diamond backsmocking across the center of the panel. Freehand embroidered flowers, flannel flower and bluebells worked in bullion lazy daisy, and wattle surround the waratah worked from the chart.

Sewing or Jewelry Roll

Degree of difficulty: Smocking easy, construction intermediate.

Requirements

Fabric for outside Pleated panel 8″ × 27½″ (20 × 70cm)

Quilted panel 8″ × 15½″ (20 × 40cm)

Lining fabric 8″ × 44½″ (20 × 112cm)

Batting: 8″ × 35½″ (20 × 90cm)

Satin bias binding: 35½″ (90cm)

Satin ribbon ¼″ wide, 20½″

Zipper 6″ (15cm)

Smocking

- Pleat the 8″ × 11½″ (20 × 70cm) panel with 19 rows of pleating.
- Tie off the pleating threads.
- Work chosen design from graph.
- Remove all except the top and bottom pleating threads.
- Block and steam the work to measure approximately 7½″ (19cm) in width plus seam allowances.
- The backsmocked center panel may be finished in a variety of ways:

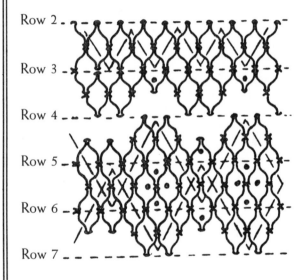

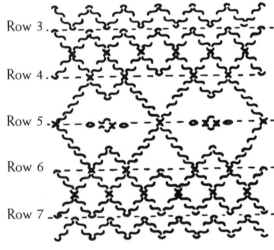

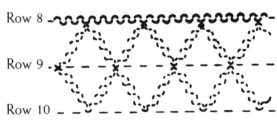

Design 1

Design 2

(a) It may be left as it is to illustrate the decorative use of backsmocking.

(b) Embroidered *after* blocking with bullion stitch, lazy daisy stitch flowers or beads.

(c) The whole area can be covered with 35mm ribbon or lace or a combination of both as shown in the photograph. Pin the ribbon and/or lace carefully over the pleated area between the two cable rows. Topstitch carefully by machine.

Assembly

- Cut a piece of batting 8″ × 17¾″ (20 × 45cm)
- Cut a piece of fabric large enough to cover the area of batting that will *not* be covered by the smocked fabric. Quilt this fabric as desired.
- Insert a tie of ³⁄₁₆″ wide ribbon (5cm), 11¾″ (30cm) long at the center point of the seam with the smocking and quilting positioned right sides together. Adjust the position of the seam so that the smocked panel covers the remainder of the batting when it is opened out.
- Stitch carefully, using a zipper foot to fit snugly against the pleats. Fold the smocked panel down over the remainder of the batting and tack carefully into place along the rows of cable backsmocking.
- Trim this panel evenly to measure 6½″ × 16½″ (17cm × 42cm).
- Cover the remaining batting with lining fabric and quilt as desired.
- Cut a second panel 6¾″ × 16½″ (17 × 42cm) for the backing and cut the remainder of the fabric to size according to the diagram for the pockets.

1 Zipper Pocket

- Fold fabric in half and press.
- Position the zipper with the fold close to the edge of the teeth. Pin in place carefully through one thickness only.
- Open out the fabric and stitch from the *back* of the zipper.

- Fold the pocket along the original fold line and tack in place on the backing panel.

2 Ribbon or Braid

- Position ribbon or braid over the other side of the zipper and topstitch in place on the zipper side only.

3 Small Pockets

- Prepare the strip for the small pockets by stitching the lining strip to the quilted strip along the top edge, taking a ³⁄₁₆″ (5mm) turning.
- Fold the lining to the back of the quilted strip forming a ³⁄₁₆″ contrast binding along the top edge. Trim the bottom edge of lining to match the quilted strip.

  The strip is positioned so that the other side of the ribbon or braid will cover the base of these pockets.

- Divide this area on the backing panel into 4 equal widths, after making allowance for the side seams.
- Measure and divide the pocket strip, allowing ³⁄₁₆″ (5mm) *extra* for each pocket plus seam allowances.
- Matching division marks and side seams, stitch down between each pocket.
- Fold the extra fullness into tiny pleats at the base of the pockets. Cover with the ribbon/braid and topstitch in place.

4 Flap Pocket

- Sew the two pieces 7″ × 5¼″ or 18 × 13.5cm (including 5-mm seam allowances) right sides together around all sides leaving a small opening near the bottom of one long side for turning.
- Clip across the corners and trim the seams if necessary. Turn and press. Fold 2⅜″ (6cm) up from the base to form a pocket and topstitch onto the backing, down the sides and along the base. This will leave a second pocket behind. Attach a fastener to the flap if desired.

5 Pin and Needle Holder

- Sew the fabric right sides together, down the 7″ (18cm) edge. Press the seam open. Turn inside out and fold with the seam down the center back. Tack in place down the side edges only.

To Finish

- Placing a second ribbon tie at the center of the other side of the smocked panel, place the two completed panels, right sides together, and sew carefully along the short ends (use the zipper foot for the smocked panel end).
- Turn right sides out, bind the side edges carefully with satin bias, stitching directly over the cable backsmocking on the smocked panel.
- Trim the seams if necessary and hand-hem the binding on the inside of the roll.

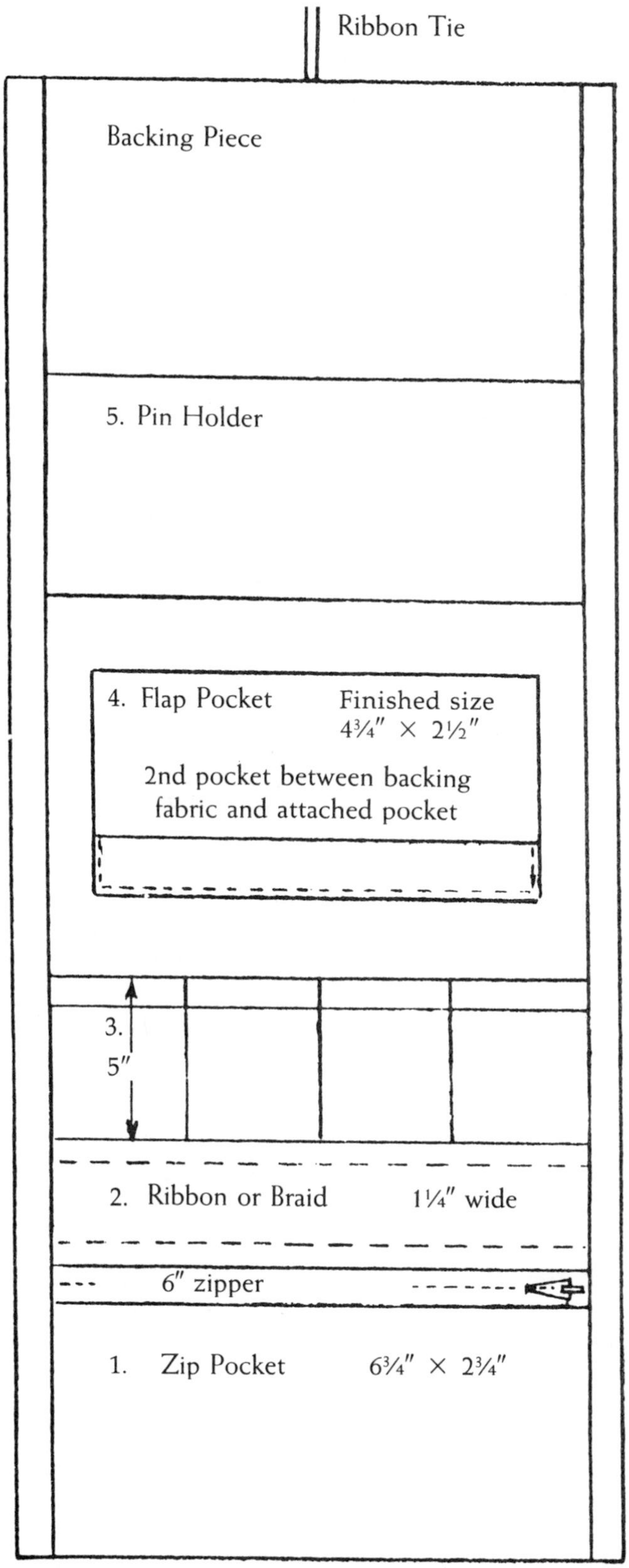

Ribbon Tie

Backing Piece

5. Pin Holder

4. Flap Pocket   Finished size
                      4¾″ × 2½″

2nd pocket between backing
fabric and attached pocket

3.

5″

2. Ribbon or Braid   1¼″ wide

6″ zipper

1.   Zip Pocket   6¾″ × 2¾″

SEWING OR JEWELRY ROLL
Pockets Diagram
Cut 1 from quilted fabric
6¾″ × 16½″

Cut 1 piece from quilted fabric
7″ × 5″

Cut 1 Quilted Piece
1 Lining Piece
7″ × 5¼″

Cut 1 Quilted Strip
8″ × 2¼″

Lining Strip
8″ × 3″

Cut 1 piece 8″ × 6″

Baby Quilt or Wall Hanging

Degree of difficulty: Smocking, intermediate stacking. Construction, Method 1 advanced, Method 2 basic.

See the general instructions for picture smocking.

Fabric requirements depend on the size of quilt to be made. The center panel of 12 blocks measures 11½″ × 15″ (29 × 38cm), including turnings. The finished size of each block is 3½″ (9cm) square.

It is most important to make the blocks a uniform size if they are to be joined together as described in construction Method 1. I therefore suggest backsmocking a trial block to estimate exactly how many pleats will be needed to create a 3½″ square.

One strip of 44″ (112cm) wide fabric 13cm (5″) deep should make 3 blocks, allowing plenty for turnings.

Fabric allowance for borders will depend on the finished size required. Lining fabric plus fine batting are also needed.

Quilting the unsmocked squares gives them enough body to support the weight of the smocked squares but the batting used should be very fine to avoid making the seams too bulky.

If desired, a second layer of batting can be used inside the quilt.

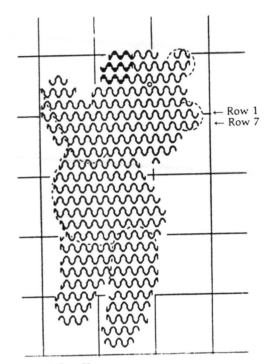

← Row 1
← Row 7

Color Key
Brown 〜〜〜
Cream 〜〜〜

Definition
5 × ½ reading from the right

SMOCKING

- Pleat and smock 6 squares, according to the charts, taking care to make the squares all the same size. *Make sure you leave all vertical seam allowances unsmocked.*
- All blocks for the quilt are backsmocked with four-step, full-space waves *before* working the surface designs.

These teddy bear designs are not difficult but they do contain a number of half-stitches (worked over a single pleat) and some alternating cables, to achieve more accurate shaping.

Follow the chart carefully, starting from the point indicated by the arrow. Work each row right across the design, using separate needles for each color block. The number of cables in each row are listed. The sitting bear and the standing bear facing *right* will be the right way up when working odd-numbered rows and upside down for even-numbered rows. The reverse applies for the standing bear facing *left*.

In each case the bears are started in the middle and worked up towards the head and then down to the feet.

Sitting Bear

Row 1—½ + 33 + ½ B
Row 2—½ + 33 + ½ B
Row 3—17 B
Row 4—4 B, 5 C, 4 B
Row 5—½ + 5 B, 7 C, 5 + ½ B
Row 6—½ + 5 + ½ B, ½ + 5 + ½ C, ½ + 5 + ½ B
Row 7—½ + 17 + ½ B
Row 8—½ + 19 + ½ B
Row 9—½ + 19 + ½ B
Row 10—3, 7, 3 B
Row 11—33 B
Row 12—½ + 19 + ½ B
Row 13—½ + 19 + ½ B
Row 14—25 B
Row 15—3 C, 29 B, 3 C
Row 16—5 C, 9 B, 7 B (alternating), 9 B, 5 C
Row 17—5 C, 8 B, 8 B, 5 C
Row 18—3 C, 6 B, 6 B, 3 C

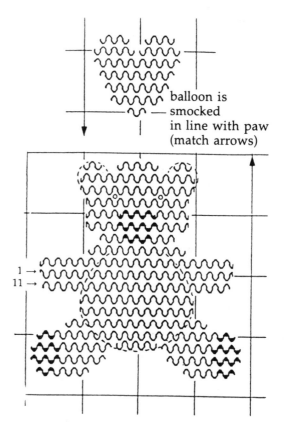

balloon is smocked in line with paw (match arrows)

Color Key
Brown
Cream
Definition
½ + 5 reading from the left

Complete features, position flowers and double flowerettes as desired. Couch the balloon string in place.

The dotted lines on the graphs indicate outline stitching worked in a single strand of dark brown to define body, arms and legs. The ears may be outlined in this way or with couched bullion stitches to give greater effect. Work the eyes with black colonial knots and the nose with straight stitches in black. For the neck bow, work two lazy daisy stitches with a fly stitch anchored across the meeting point of the lazy daisy stitches.

Standing Bear

Row 1—27 + ½ B
Row 2—½ + 8, ½ + 17 B
Row 3—16 + ½, ½ + 5 + ½ B
Row 4—3 B, 5 C, 10 B
Row 5—½ + 9 + ½ B, ½ + 5 C
Row 6—½ + 3 + ½ C, ½ + 4 B, 2 + ½ B
Row 7—26 + ½ B
Row 8—½ + 22 B
Row 9—19 + ½ B
Row 10—½ + 13 + ½, 1 B
Row 11—½ + 15 + ½ B
Row 12—½ + 17 B
Row 13—18 + ½ B
Row 14—½ + 19 B
Row 15—18 + ½ B
Row 16—½, ½ + 16 B
Row 17—½ + 16 + ½ B
Row 18—½ + 16 + ½,B
Row 19—½ + 16 + ½ B
Row 20—½ + 7, 8 + ½ B
Row 21—½ + 7, ½ + 6 + ½ B
Row 22—½ + 5 + ½, ½ + 7 B
Row 23—½ + 6 + ½, 5 B
Row 24—½ + 6 B
Row 25—5 B

Threads

Soi d'Alger (used for original design)
Cream 4241   Brown 4611
DMC
Cream 739   Brown 3064

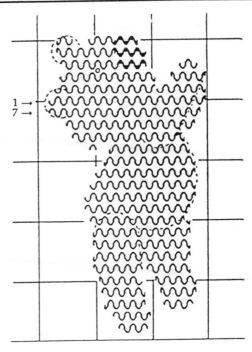

Color Key
Brown 〰〰〰
Cream 〰〰〰
Definition
½ + 5 reading from the left

Kite Block

Work the outline in stem and outline stitch as indicated on the chart. Fill in with 3 more rows, working as close as possible to each preceding row. Work a small heart in the center. The tail is worked freehand in stem stitch with the addition of decorative bows worked as described. The kite string is added after the assembly of the quilt, using a fine couched thread.

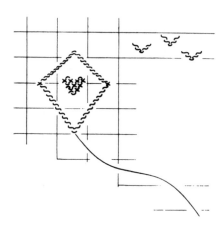

- Position the smocked squares onto the quilt top, trimming as required and so as to leave ⅛" seam allowance. Tack into place carefully.
- Sew the squares to the quilt top using a ³⁄₁₆" ribbon or braid to cover the raw edges.
- Finish quilt as before.

ASSEMBLY

Method 1

- Remove pleating threads and block squares very carefully.
- Quilt enough fabric to cut 6 squares each 4¼" (11cm) square.
- *In order for the seams to lie smoothly, it is vital that piecing be done vertically, according to the diagram.*
- Add borders to achieve desired size.
- Tack the front, batting and backing together.
- Quilt through all thicknesses between the blocks by hand or machine if desired.
- Bind the edges as required.

Method 2

- Cut one piece of fabric and one piece of batting the required size of the completed quilt plus turning. Tack both pieces together.

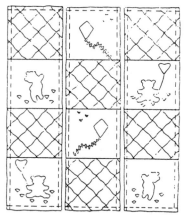

**Make three strips
each of four squares**

It is not necessary to use as many squares for this method as they can be arranged in any formation.

The large ABC panel illustrated could also be used as a panel for a quilt.

Picture Panels

Degree of difficulty: Advanced.

Two ideas for smocked pictures are shown in color.

The ABC picture panel uses the design given on the following page, together with the teddy bears from the quilt design. It is not difficult to do if the panel is backsmocked, blocked and steamed before commencing the design.

Start by working the vertical lines of the blocks in satin stitch over two pleats. The top and bottom lines of the blocks can then be drawn in with a ruler and marking pen.

These lines are worked with 2 closely positioned rows of outline or stem stitch, whichever sits best.

The teddy pictured is a Gund Kinder Bear.

Numbers on arrows indicate the number of pleats between each vertical line.

Note. Leave lines that touch the bears until after they have been worked, count the pleats for the standing bear carefully to ensure the paws finish on the pleat next to the corner of the top block.

The outlines for the letters are drawn in with a marking pen, using a ruler where applicable. The letters are then finished with a combination of satin stitch, outline and stem stitch.

The design for the wren picture has been included to show how attractive a fabric-covered frame can be for this type of work, as it offers the opportunity of coordinating the frame with the design of the picture. In this case the wattle is embroidered with silk ribbon both on the frame and the smocking.

I find the most satisfactory way of mounting smocking for framing is to make a very snug fitting bag into which you place the cardboard backing section of the frame, slipstitch the opening, firmly stretching the fabric around the card. This gives a firm backing onto which you can stretch and sew the smocked panel, carefully lining up the pleats as you work.

Glue the covered front panel in place carefully and fill the gap between the two sections with a decorative cord edging.

Bibs and Bootees

Degree of difficulty: Smocking easy. Assembly—Teddy bib, very easy. Christening bib and bootees, intermediate.

BOOTEES

The bootees pictured are made from a 6″ (15-cm) wide Swiss lace edging. However, they can be cut from any lightweight fabric and finished with a lace edging.

Requirements

Strip of fabric 5″ × 37¾″ (13 × 96cm)
Small piece of interfacing for sole
Satin ribbon 1/16″ wide, 29½″ (75cm)

Smocking

Pleat bootees as indicated on the pattern and smock according to the chart.

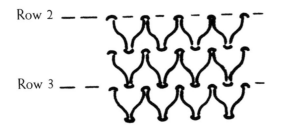

Row 1

Row 2

Row 3

Row 4

Bootee

Assembly

- Remove the pleating threads and work any further embroidery as desired; for example, bullion rosebuds or shadow-stitch bows on the toe.
- Join the center-back seam with a tiny French seam.
- Prepare the sole by layering a piece of interfacing between two layers of fabric. Refer to diagrams for the easiest and most accurate way to do this.
- Gather the lower edge of bootee and adjust to fit the sole.
- Stitch carefully, along the sole seam line with right sides together.
- Neaten seam with zigzag stitching trimming if necessary.
- Thread ribbon through the first row of chevron, using a tapestry needle, commencing at the center front.

CHRISTENING BIB

A practical gift for baby, pretty enough to be worn on any special occasion. This bib can be made from voile in soft pastel shades or in a particular fabric to match baby's clothes.

Requirements

Piece of fabric 15¾″ × 39½″ (40 × 100cm)
Bias strip or satin bias for neck

Method

- Make a pattern template, using firm paper or heavy vilene as indicated on the pattern.
- Fold the fabric in half, right sides together, to measure 8 × 39½″ (20 × 100cm).

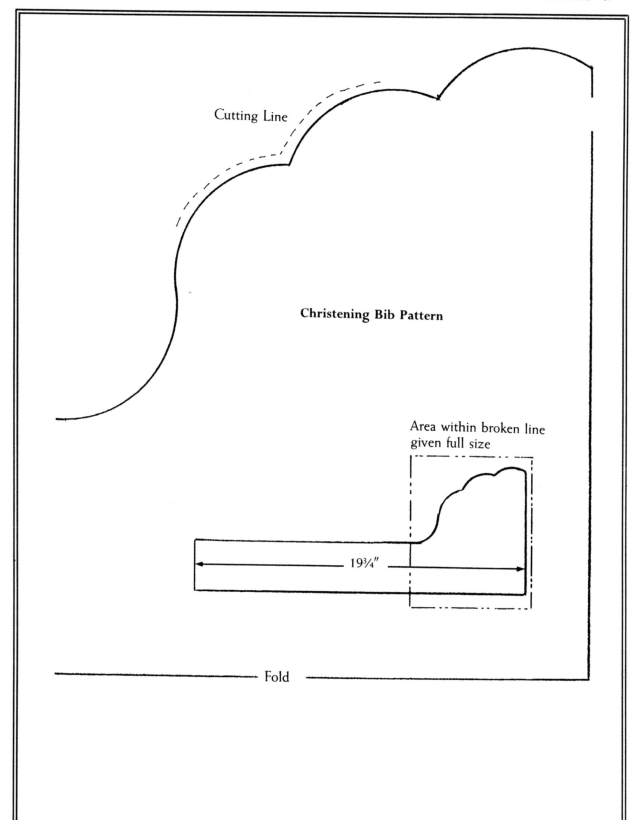

Cutting Line

Christening Bib Pattern

Area within broken line
given full size

19¾"

Fold

- Position the pattern on the fabric. Using a fadable pen and drawing very lightly, mark the lower edge outline of the pattern onto the fabric.
- Machine-stitch along the marked line, carefully working around the scallops.
- Trim the edge leaving a ³⁄₁₆" (5-mm) seam allowance. Clip into the corners of the scallops. Turn and press.
- Work any additional embroidery required around the scalloped edge *before* pleating.
- Press and tack both layers together along the top edge.
- Pleat the neck edge through both thicknesses with 4 full rows or 8 half-rows of pleating.
- Smock with the given design.
- Remove all except the neck edge pleating thread.
- Adjust the neckline to the required measurement, approximately 11¼"–11¾" (28 to 30cm). Block and steam into shape.
- Turn in the back edges and hand-sew in place.
- Bind the neck edge with a bias strip cut to size.
- Fasten with ribbon ties or a button and loop fastening.

TEDDY'S BIB

To fit a bear, measuring approximately 18cm (7") around the neck.

A charming addition to baby's first teddy, this little bib, worked from the bootee pattern, is very quick and easy to make.

Requirements

Strip of fabric 4¾" × 37¾" (12 × 96cm)

Method

- Cut and pleat as indicated on the pattern.
- Finish the top and bottom edges as desired.
- Smock according to the chart.
- Remove the pleating threads.
- Hem the short back edges.
- Thread with ribbon at the neckline.

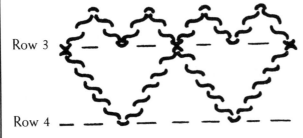

Baby Bib

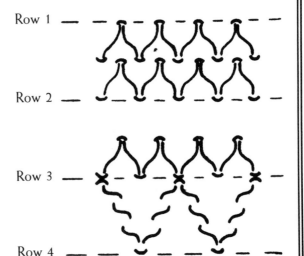

Teddy Bib

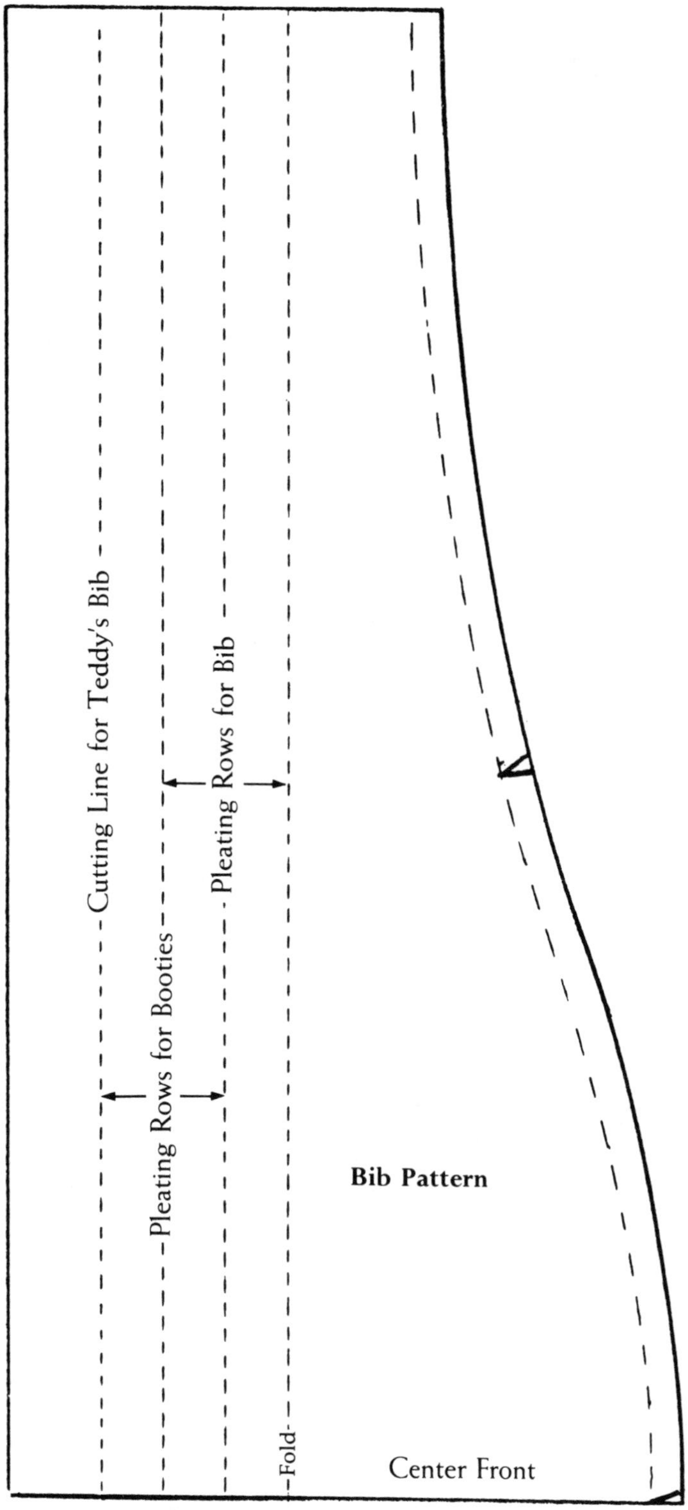

Cutting Line for Teddy's Bib

Pleating Rows for Booties

Pleating Rows for Bib

Bib Pattern

Fold

Center Front

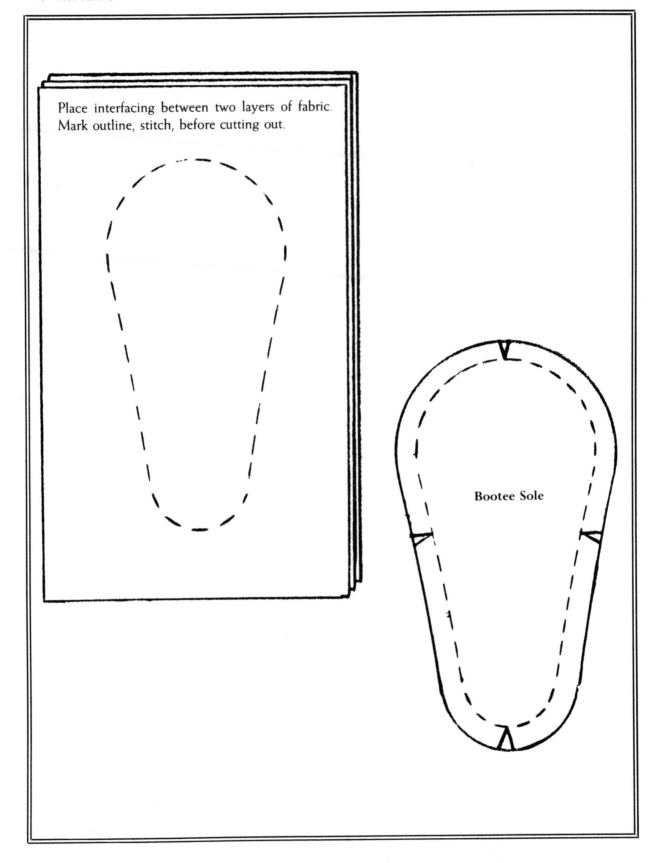

Place interfacing between two layers of fabric.
Mark outline, stitch, before cutting out.

Bootee Sole

Christmas Decorations

Degree of difficulty: Smocking very easy, construction easy.

Dress up your tree with these quick and easy decorations. They can also be used as decorative containers for extra special little gifts.

Any simple combination of cable, wave or chevron stitches can be used. Chevron combinations will allow experimentation with ribbon threading. The addition of beads or sequins adds variety and sparkle to your designs, as will the use of silver, gold or colored filament threads in combination with the regular smocking threads.

The patterns given are for small decorations but it is very easy to enlarge them.

CHRISTMAS STOCKINGS

Fabric Requirements

For stocking suitable cotton fabric
For decorative frill (approximately 1"-wide finished size) 13½" (35-cm) cotton voile, cotton lace edging or ribbon

Smocking

- If using voile, finish the bottom edge. Ribbon and cotton lace edging require no finishing. The top edge of the frill can be turned under and pleated double.
- Pleat and smock the frill.
- Remove the pleating threads.

Row 1

Row 2

Row 3 – – – – – – – – – – – –

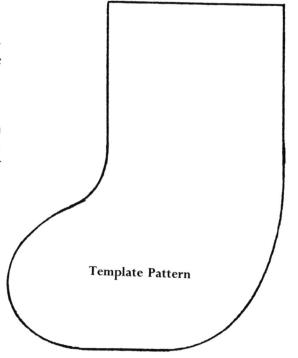

Template Pattern

Assembly

- Make a firm template of the stocking pattern.
- Fold the fabric in half right sides together. Place the template on the fabric, allowing room for the seam allowance and carefully draw around it.
- Stitch around the marked line. Cut out the stocking, allowing 5-mm seam *outside* the stitching.
- Turn right sides out. Turn a narrow hem to the *outside* around the top.
- Sew the smocked cuff right sides together, joining the short ends, slip over the top of the stocking and hand-stitch in place.
- Thread with ribbon and sew on beads as required. Ribbon threaded through the top row can be started at the center back and the ends knotted into a hanging loop.
    A second row of ribbon started on the side can be finished by looping the ends into a bow and stitching in place with a tiny bead.
- Stuff the lower part of the stocking and fill the top with a tiny toy or package.

CHRISTMAS PARTY SNAPPERS

Based on a cardboard tube 3cm in diameter by 8 cm long.

Fabric Requirements

A piece of voile 6″ × 13¾″ (15 × 35cm)
Lace edging 27½″ (70 cm)

Method

- Finish both long edges of the fabric with lace edging. This is not difficult to do after smocking is completed, if preferred.
- Center 10 rows of pleating across the fabric.
- Work the required smocking design from Rows 3 to 8 *only*.
- Remove all except the top and bottom pleating threads.

- Join the seam carefully. Slip the cardboard tube inside and using the remaining pleating threads, tie the fabric firmly in place.
- Decorate with ribbon and beads.

To increase the size of this design allow 3 times the circumference of the support tube for the fabric width. When calculating the length remember that pulling the fabric in around the ends of the tube requires extra pleating threads at either end of the smocked panel. The number of threads depends on the diameter of the tube used.

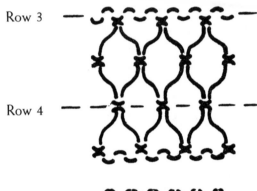

Row 3

Row 4

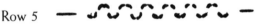

Row 5

Row 6

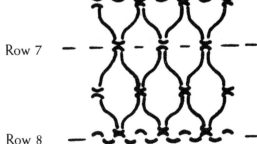

Row 7

Row 8

CHRISTMAS BELL

Requirements

Strip of fabric 3″ (8cm)
Circle of fabric 3½″ (9cm) in diameter for each bell
A styrofoam bell form 2½″ (6.5cm) across the base and 6.5cm deep
Ribbon and beads for trimming
3 pearl pins for attaching ribbon and clapper

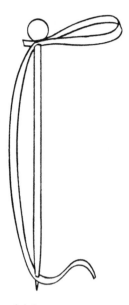

Making a rosette

Row 1

Row 2

Row 3

Row 4

Row 5

Row 6

Row 7

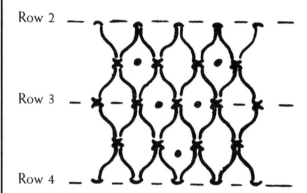

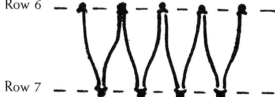

Bell

Pleating

Finish the bottom edge of the fabric. Pleat with 7 rows of pleating, commencing the bottom row 1 cm from the lower edge.

Smocking

- Work 70 pleats for each bell, smocking the design given.
- Remove all except the top pleating thread and sew on beads as desired.

Construction

- To cover the bell base, run a strong gathering thread around the edge of the fabric circle and place it over the base of the bell. Pull up around the base and secure the gathering thread firmly.
- Hand-stitch the smocking into a tube, matching the design.
- Place over the bell and hold firmly in place around the base with pins while pulling up and tying off pleating thread number one.
- Thread ribbon through the first row of full-space chevron and adjust to fit. Loop the ends into a simulated bow securing at the center point with a pearl-headed pin.

- Use fabric glue sparingly to attach the frilled edge around the bottom of the bell.
- Make a ribbon rosette on a long pin to decorate the top and attach with fabric glue.
- Use another pearl-headed pin in the base for the clapper.

To make a ribbon rosette use ribbon ⅛″ (3mm) wide and push a pearl-headed pin through the ribbon ³⁄₁₆″ (5mm) from one end. Using the length of the pin as a measurement guide, push the ribbon onto the pin a pin's length away from the first pick up. Slide to the head of the pin to form a loop. Repeat for a total of 8 loops, trim the end close to the pin. Place a dot of glue under the rosette and press the pin into the bell top. Arrange the loops evenly to form a rosette.

Baby Gown or Dress

(Size: Birth to six months)

FABRIC REQUIREMENTS

29½" of 44" wide fabric (75cm of 112cm)

SUITABLE FABRICS

Voile, fine cotton, winter weight cotton, Clydella or fine knit fabric.

PATTERN

Fold the fabric in half, divide and cut into panels. Cut a bias strip for the neck binding 10½" × 1½" (27cm × 4.5cm). Mark the armhole cutting line onto each panel as shown using the pattern guide.

METHOD

- Finish the cuff edge of the sleeves.
- Pleat the front and back panel with 7 rows of pleating.
- Pleat the sleeve cuff with 4 rows of pleating.
- Smock the front, back and sleeves with any bishop design of your choice.
- Remove pleating threads except for the top-neck thread which should be pulled back to the armhole cutting line.
- Cut out armhole shaping.
- Block smocking to shape.
- Machine-gather top of sleeve.
- Sew sleeves to the front and back at armhole using a narrow open seam, French seam or overlocked seam.
- Using a flat open seam sew center-back seam, leaving 10cm (4") open at the top for neck opening. Press seam open and tack in place at the neckline.
- Prepare bias binding. Adjust gathers and pleats evenly to fit the bias strip, leaving a 5mm overlap at the back edges. Stitch along the top pleating thread.
- Trim seam, turn in back overlap, fold bias strip to inside and hem carefully in place. *Note:* If using knit fabric, bind neck with a straight strip of fabric approximately 1" × 9" (2.5cm × 23cm), according to stretch. Overlock one edge, stretch onto neck adjusting gathers to 10¼" (26cm). Finish as above.
- Sew side and sleeve seams.
- Finish bottom edge with lace edging or hem to the desired length.

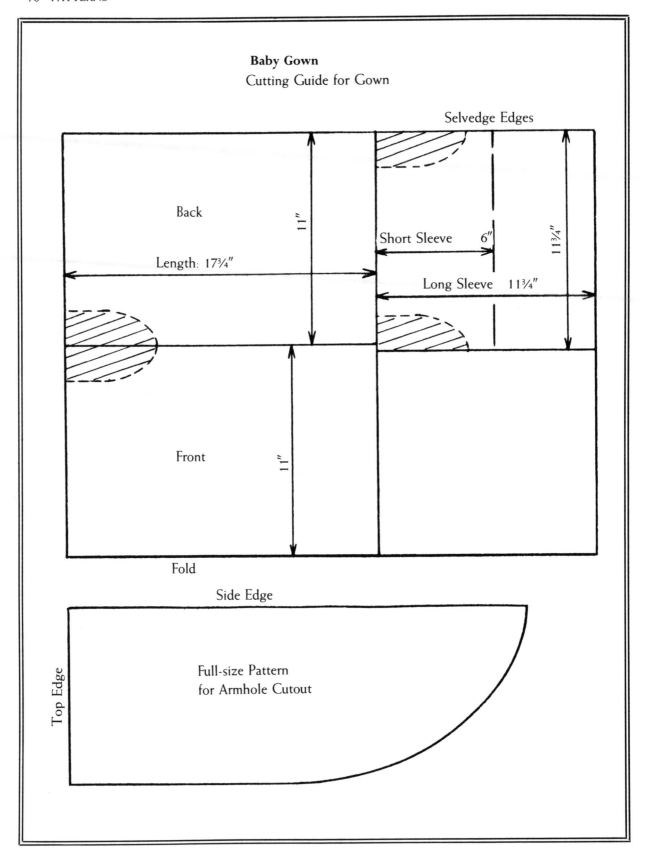

Baby Gown
Cutting Guide for Gown

Selvedge Edges

Back

11″

Length: 17¾″

Short Sleeve   6″

11¾″

Long Sleeve   11¾″

Front

11″

Fold

Side Edge

Top Edge

Full-size Pattern
for Armhole Cutout

Bishop Simplicity

Size: Teddy to Adult

This is a lovely ruffled sleeve, bishop style dress or nightgown, which is cleverly designed to reduce sewing to the very minimum. Pleating is easy as there are no seams in the smocked area and ribbon holds the neckline in place, dispensing with the need to bind the neck. Finally construction after the smocking is finished only involves 3 straight seams and the hem.

Cutting out is simple and easier still if you own a cutting board on which to lay out the fabric.

All sizes except the teddy dresses are cut sideways along the fabric, so make sure the fabric design looks right this way around. The design is ideal for border prints. 35½" (90cm) wide fabric is sufficient for a short length gown in adult sizes. Note, however, that it is not possible to vary the sleeve style of this pattern and that, unless extra wide fabric can be purchased, it is necessary to add a frill to the bottom of the adult sizes to make a full length gown.

Size	Fabric		Measurements		Armhole cutout number	Number of pleating threads
	Length	Width	X	Y		
Small Teddy	6¼	30¾	5	1½	1	3
Large Teddy	8¼	45	7½	2¼	2	3
6 to 12 months	71	15¾	11¾	2¾	2	4
2 years	83	17¾ or as required	13¾	3½	2	5
4 years	95	19¾ or as required	15¾	4¼	3	5
6 years	101	as required	16½	5	3	8
8 to 10 years	104	as required	17½	5	3	8
12 to 14 years & 6 to 8 adult	109	35½ to 45	18	5½	4	8
10 to 14 adult	118	35½ to 45	19¾	6	5	8
16 to 18 adult	130	35½ to 45	21¾	6¼	5	8

All measurements are in inches.
For centimeter equivalents refer to chart.

METHOD

- Cut out garment according to the pattern layout, using the measurements from the chart appropriate to the size required. Select corresponding armhole pattern and trace onto the fabric at the top of the underarm cutout panel (see dotted lines on diagram). Cut out this shaping.
- Roll-hem the top neck edge and armhole frill marked from A to A on the diagram.
- Pleat the top edge with required number of pleating threads.
- Smock with given design or any bishop design, remembering that the design chosen must allow for ribbon insertion at the neck edge.
- Remove pleating threads.
- Center the back seam. This may be closed completely on the larger sizes, taking care to match the pattern. Children's sizes up to age four will need a small opening left at the center back to allow enough room for their heads to pass through.
- Commence the seam immediately below the smocked design, using a flat open seam, turn the remaining seam allowance back onto smocking and stitch lightly into place. Close with tiny buttons and loops.
- Thread ribbon under the smocking stitches using a tapestry needle. Start from the center back if an opening has been left there or from the front for adult sizes.
- Tack the side seams in order to try on the garment. Adjust neckline, tie or sew ribbon securely.
- Remove side tacking and block smocking by pinning out and adjusting the neckline into a circle. Pin the smocking out evenly into a circle and steam gently.
- Stitch side seams.
- Adjust length and hem as desired.

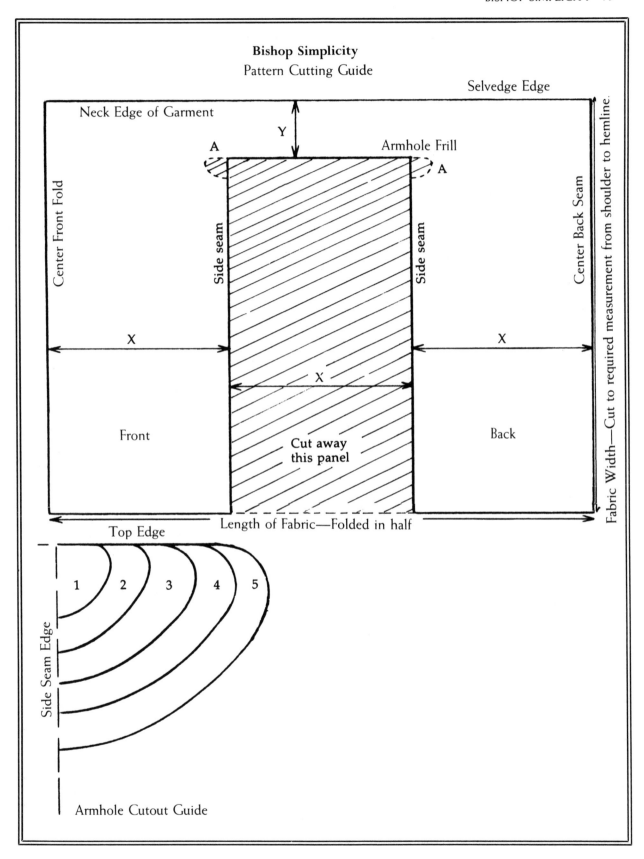

Bishop Simplicity
Pattern Cutting Guide

Selvedge Edge

Neck Edge of Garment

Y

A

Armhole Frill

A

Center Front Fold

Side seam

Side seam

Center Back Seam

X

X

X

Front

Cut away
this panel

Back

Fabric Width—Cut to required measurement from shoulder to hemline.

Top Edge

Length of Fabric—Folded in half

Side Seam Edge

1 2 3 4 5

Armhole Cutout Guide

Collars

A smocked collar piece can be used in a variety of ways. A detachable collar may be used to add a special touch to a plain sweater or dress. They make very acceptable gifts and are suitable for any age group. It is easy to substitute a smocked collar for the regular collar on a favorite dress or blouse pattern.

A collar piece can also be used to overlay the yoke of a dress or blouse constructed from a pattern, where the yoke is cut to form a circle.

The table on page 81 gives the amount of fabric required for collars of all sizes, taking into account the following factors:

- Fabric recommended—voile, batiste or organdy, all of which require finishing with lace edging, a decorative machine edging or with hand-rolling and whipping. Swiss embroidered lace 5"–6" (12–15cm) wide is a perfect alternative but care should be taken to choose a design that is not too heavily embroidered and where the pattern is limited to the outer edge of the fabric. Narrower 2"–3" (5–8cm) laces can be used for infants, dolls and teddy bears.
- The design to be smocked on the collar has a direct effect on the amount of fabric required. Van Dyke stitch designs require less fabric and the collar will therefore not be as full and fluffy when worn. A full collar can look lovely on dolls, teddy bears and young children but may look overdone on an adult.

    Miniaturizing a design by working it on half-space pleating restricts the elasticity of the smocking considerably. This results in greater fabric requirements than might be expected for dolls and teddy bears.
- The depth of the smocking design on the collar piece also affects the fabric requirements. The deeper the smocking design the greater the fabric requirement.

The finished depth of the collar piece can be a matter of personal choice; however most collars of this type are made to the measurement taken from the collar line to the point of the shoulder.

Dolls and teddy bears rarely have much shoulder line and their collars can be made to extend beyond this point if desired.

For most collars the smocked design should not extend beyond half the width of the finished collar.

PREPARATION

Where possible, cut the collar fabric as a single piece, taking a strip from the side of the fabric down the selvedge. Swiss batiste and voile is available as 55" or 59" (140cm or 150cm) fabric in some shops.

The easiest way to finish the neck edge of a collar, particularly on miniature sizes, is with a rolled hem or lace edging. Smock close to this edge, using a stitch suitable for ribbon insertion. After smocking, thread the top row with a narrow ribbon adjusting it to the required neck measurement before stitching the ends securely. Fasten the collar with tiny buttons and loops.

The bottom edge of the collar should be finished before pleating using one of the methods described. Note that collars do not always need a lace edging. To make an inexpensive collar for a child's dress, experiment with the fancy edging stitches on your sewing machine or use contrasting thread for the rolled-hem edge on the overlocker.

MAKING

- Pleat and smock in a straight piece, using a bishop style design of your choice, leaving one pleating thread at the top edge unsmocked if the collar is to be attached to a garment or finished with a bias neck binding.

- Remove pleating threads *except neckline thread.* Tie this thread to the required neck measurement or, if a neckline ruffle edge is used, thread ribbon and adjust it to the required measurement.
- Block the collar by pinning the neck firmly into a circle. Stretch the design out, pinning it evenly at the points of the design. Steam carefully until the design lies flat when the pins are removed.

FINISHING

Detachable collars may be finished with a ruffle as previously described or with a bias neck binding. A lining yoke may be attached under the neck binding to be worn inside the garment in order to hold the collar in place more securely. This lining piece can be cut to match the shape of the collar or from the yoke of a suitable dress or blouse pattern.

To attach a collar to a garment after smocking, adjust the neck thread of the collar to the neck measurement of the garment, tack in place and bind the neck with a bias strip cut to neck size.

A collar can also be used on a garment with a mandarin or stand-up collar. Tack the collar to the neckline of the bodice before attaching the pattern collar piece as directed in the pattern.

If the collar piece is to form the yoke of the garment, work a collar piece to match the yoke section of the pattern. Cut a lining from the yoke pattern. Join the shoulder seams. Block the smocked collar to match the yoke lining. Attach the collar with bias binding at the neckline. Hand-sew the collar piece over the yoke seam line or attach to the yoke by embroidering with grub roses as embroidered on the brunch coat illustrated.

Widths and lengths are in inches. For centimeter equivalents refer to chart.

To calculate requirements for dolls and teddy bears in other sizes, allow 5 to 6 times the neck measurement for half-space Van Dyke designs and 6 to 7 times the neck measurement for other designs worked on half-space pleating.

Fabric requirements for smocked collars

	Rows of Smocking	Fabric width	Fabric length	
			Van Dyke stitch	Other stitches
Child's collar				
—to age 8 years	4 to 6	3 to 6	43¼ to 51	51 to 59
—8 to 12 years	6 to 8	5 to 6	51 to 55	59 to 67
Adult collar	8	5 to 6	59 to 63	69 to 79
Adult collar or yoke	12 to 16	5 to 6	85 to 91	118 to 130
Teddy or Doll—to fit 7–8" neck	9 half space	2¾	44	55

DESIGN PLATES

Rebecca

Design plate for baby day gown

This design *must* be centered and is worked over 76 pleats. Half-space pleating threads between rows 3 and 8 will make spacing easier for beginners.

- Commence design on row 4 with a top-level cable over the center 2 pleats (see arrow). Work one bottom-level cable, a half-space chevron up to row 3½, 3 cables followed by a half-space chevron down to row 4. Repeat to the end of the row. Return to the center, turn work and complete the row (9 pattern repeats).
- Repeat this design between rows 4 to 8, starting and finishing each row half a repeat in from the end of the previous row.

- Row 3—Cable, commencing with a bottom-level cable.
  Row 2—Cable, commencing with a top-level cable.
- Work double flowerettes or bullion rosebuds on row 2½.
- Row 1—Backsmock with cable.
- To smock the back, work half the full pattern on each side of the back opening.
- Sleeves—work rows 2 to 3 or 3½ to 4½ from the graph.

The original design was worked with 2 strands of Marlitt thread.

Pale pink 1213   pink 1207   pale green 895.

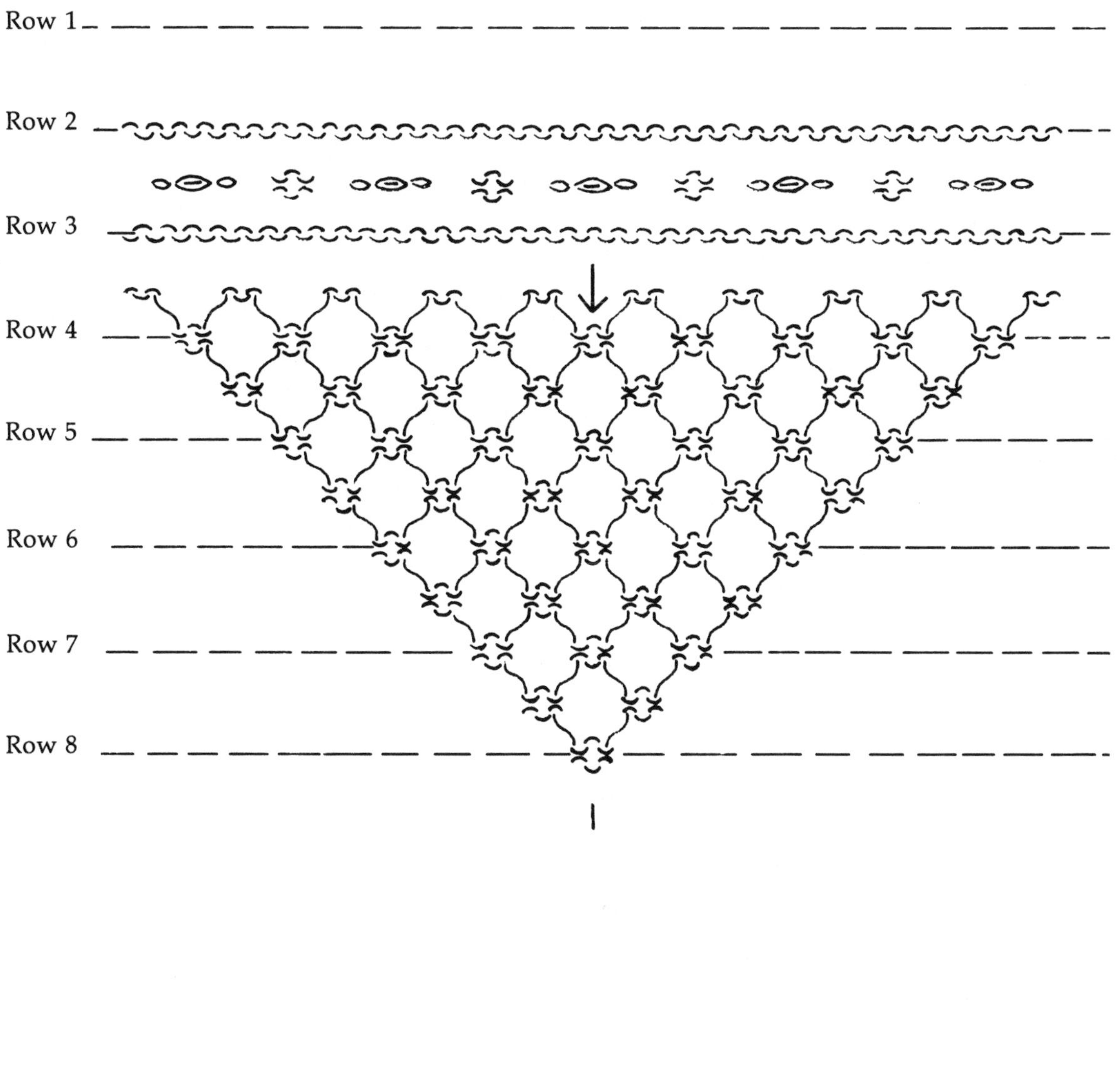

Row 1

Row 2

Row 3

Row 4

Row 5

Row 6

Row 7

Row 8

Ribbons

Design plate for Bishop Simplicity.
This pattern requires adjusting for the various sizes.
Size 6 years and up—7½ rows
Size 2 & 4 years—Rows 1 and 4 to 6½ only.
6 to 12 months—Rows 1 and 4 to 6 only.
Teddy bear—Rows 1 and 5 to 6 only.

This design should be centered.

- Commence design on row 4 with a bottom-level cable over the center 2 pleats (see arrow). Work a half-space chevron up to row 3½ and back to row 4. Continue working repeats of 5 cables 2 half-space chevrons to the end of the row, commencing each block of cables with a bottom level stitch. Return to the center, turn work and complete the row.
- Rows 4½ & 5—Work 2 rows, each shadowing the previous row.
- Rows 5 to 6—Work a half-space chevron down to row 5½ below the 5 cable stitches followed by a 3-step, full-space trellis below the 2 chevrons.
- Row 5½ to 6½—1 row, shadowing the previous row.
- Row 6 to 7½—5-step, 1½-space trellis, working the top-level cable of this row directly below the bottom-level cable of the *chevron* on the previous row.
- Row 2, 2½ and 3—3 rows of half-space chevrons.
- Row 1—Cable.
- With a tapestry needle thread 2mm ribbon through the chevrons in rows 2, 3, 4 and 5.

Original design worked with 2 strands of Marlitt thread.
  Pink 830   green 1058.

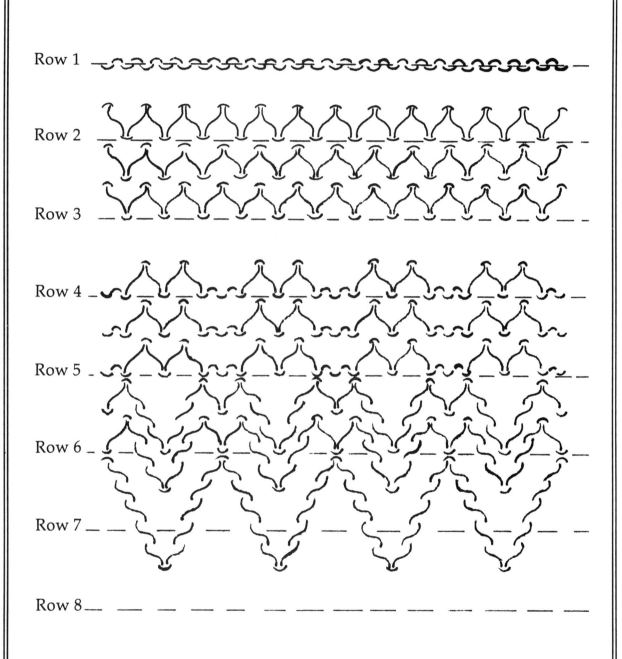

Row 1

Row 2

Row 3

Row 4

Row 5

Row 6

Row 7

Row 8

Van Dyke Collar

This design may be adapted by adding rows for wider collar pieces or omitting rows where necessary for narrow collars.

There is no need to center this design, if you are prepared to drop a few pleats from the end of the row in order to finish at the end of a full-pattern repeat.

- Commence design on row 4 (see arrow). Work half-space Van Dyke stitch down to row 6 and back to row 4. Repeat across the row.
- Rows 5 to 7 and 6 to 8—Shadow the previous row.
- Row 3 to 4—Commencing on row 4, work a row of single-space, half-step Van Dyke stitches up to row 3 and back.
- Row 2 to 3—Repeat the previous row between rows 2 and 3.
- Row 1—Backsmock with cable if required.

2 or 3mm ribbon may be threaded through the stitches between row 2 and 2½ using a tapestry needle. If this is to be used to control the neckline, move the whole pattern up one row, commencing the design on row 3.

The original designs were worked with a single strand of Marlitt thread using three shades of a single color.

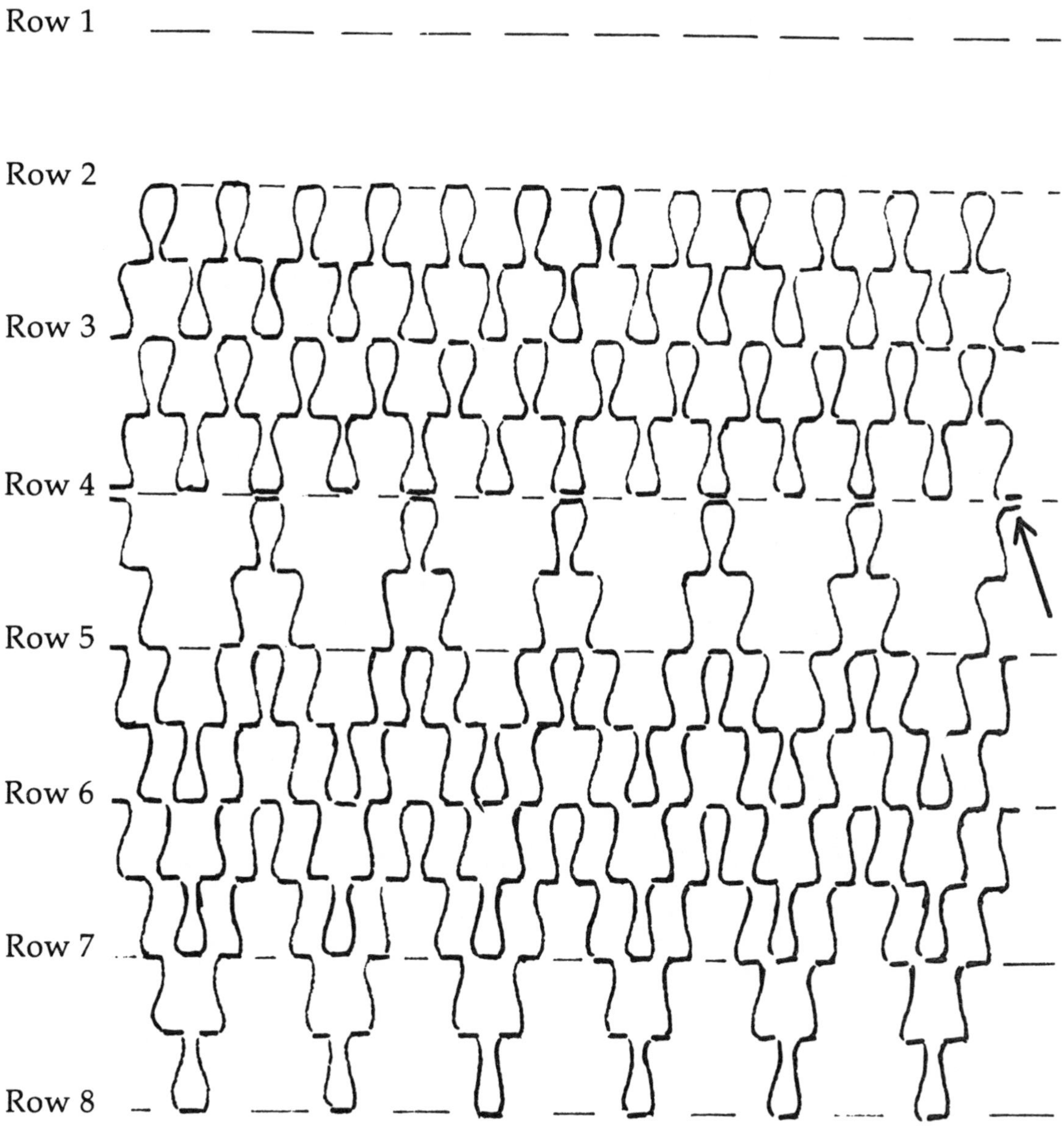

Row 1

Row 2

Row 3

Row 4

Row 5

Row 6

Row 7

Row 8

Stacking Designs

Both the designs given here contain some half-stitches (worked over a single pleat) and some alternating cables to maintain more accurate shaping.

The Wombat design is an easy stacking design.

The Blue Wren design is much more advanced with several colors being used throughout.

I suggest you backsmock the panel first; it gives a more even result and is quicker than working around the knots and threads later.

WOMBAT

Follow the chart carefully, starting from the point indicated by the arrow and using two separate needles for the dark brown stitches. The number of cables worked in each row are listed below. The wombat on the top of the chart will be the right way up when working odd-numbered rows and upside down for even-numbered rows. The reverse applies for the second wombat.

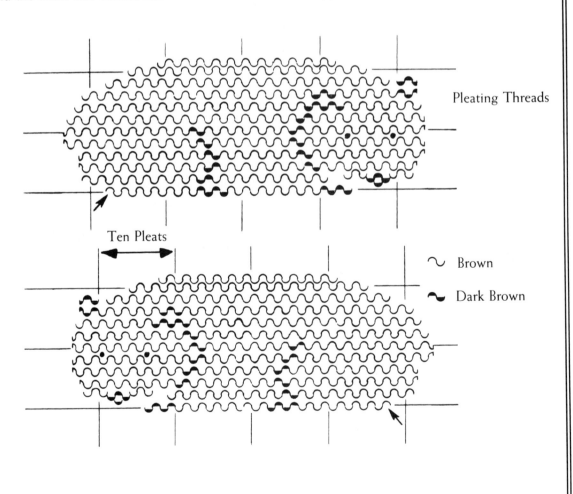

Pleating Threads

Ten Pleats

∼ Brown

∼ Dark Brown

The wombat has been worked using 4 strands of DMC thread mixing three shades of brown to achieve a more realistic color.
DMC colors used.
(B) Brown 640–2 strands
       642–1 strand
       3023–1 strand
       (DB) Dark Brown 3031
       Bright Red 666
       Green 3053

Row 1—12 B, 4 DB, 12 B, 4 DB
Row 2—15 B, 2 DB, 15 B
Row 3—½ + 16 B, 2 DB, 11 B, 2 DB, 12½ B
Row 4—½ + 14 B, 2 DB, 10 B, 2 DB, 16½ B
Row 5—½ + 17 B, 2 DB, 10 B, 2 DB, 15½ B
Row 6—½ + 15 B, 2 DB, 11 B, 2 DB, 16½ B
Row 7—30 B, 2 DB, 14½ B
Row 8—10 B, 5 DB, 30 B
Row 9—30 B, 3 DB, 8 B, 2½ DB
Row 10—½ + 2 DB, 37 B
Row 11—31 B
Row 12—23 B (alternating cables)

Complete the nose area by working 3 alternating cables in B, single flowerettes in DB and 3 alternating cables in B. Work eyes in black using a French or colonial knot. Use a single strand of white to highlight the eye with a straight stitch across one half of the knot.

BLUE WRENS

- Very careful attention to the graph is necessary when working this design as there are many color changes.
- Use 3 strands of DMC thread unless otherwise specified.
- Backsmock the panel first.

Wrens

- Follow the diagram, starting from the point indicated by the arrow. The number of cables worked in each row are listed below. The wren on the right side of the picture will be the right way up when working odd numbered rows and upside down for even-numbered rows. The reverse applies for the wren on the left.

Row 1—7 C
Row 2—13 C
Row 3—8 C, 10 N
Row 4—10 N, 3 C, 3 K
Row 5—4 K, 1 B, 1 C, 3 T, 5 N
Row 6—8 T, 3 B, 3½ K
Row 7—½ + 3 K, 1 B, 6 K, 4 B
Row 8—2 K, 3 B, 2 K, 2 B, 2½ K
Row 9—3 K, 9 B
Row 10—9 B
Row 11—5 B (alternating cables)

Tails

Using 2 strands of blue, work 3 rows of stem stitch, keeping the stitches as close as possible.

Eye

French or colonial knot in black highlighted with a white stitch.

Beak and Legs

Straight stitch in black.

Wattle

Stitch placement may be copied from the chart; however, I suggest using a fadable pen to mark in the position of the branches. Using 3 strands of brown, work outline-stitch over the marked lines. Add single flowerettes in yellow for wattle and lazy daisy leaves in green.

(B) Blue 825   (N) Brown 3032   (K) Black 301
(T) Tan 925   (C) Cream 3033   Yellow 973
               Green 3053

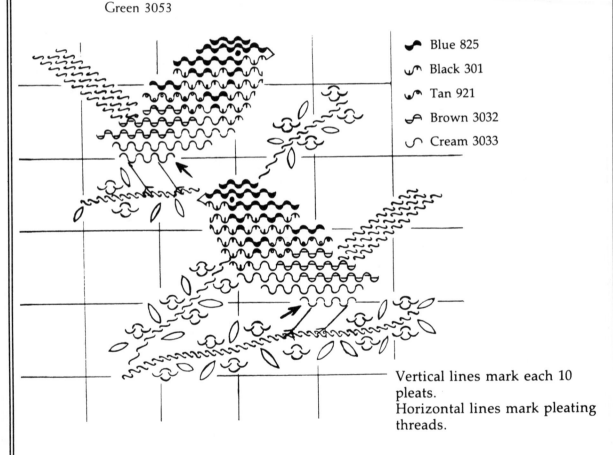

- Blue 825
- Black 301
- Tan 921
- Brown 3032
- Cream 3033

Vertical lines mark each 10 pleats.
Horizontal lines mark pleating threads.

METRIC EQUIVALENCY CHART

MM—MILLIMETRES   CM—CENTIMETRES

INCHES TO MILLIMETRES AND CENTIMETRES

INCHES	MM	CM	INCHES	CM	INCHES	CM
⅛	3	0.3	9	22.9	30	76.2
¼	6	0.6	10	25.4	31	78.7
⅜	10	1.0	11	27.9	32	81.3
½	13	1.3	12	30.5	33	83.8
⅝	16	1.6	13	33.0	34	86.4
¾	19	1.9	14	35.6	35	88.9
⅞	22	2.2	15	38.1	36	91.4
1	25	2.5	16	40.6	37	94.0
1¼	32	3.2	17	43.2	38	96.5
1½	38	3.8	18	45.7	39	99.1
1¾	44	4.4	19	48.3	40	101.6
2	51	5.1	20	50.8	41	104.1
2½	64	6.4	21	53.3	42	106.7
3	76	7.6	22	55.9	43	109.2
3½	89	8.9	23	58.4	44	111.8
4	102	10.2	24	61.0	45	114.3
4½	114	11.4	25	63.5	46	116.8
5	127	12.7	26	66.0	47	119.4
6	152	15.2	27	68.6	48	121.9
7	178	17.8	28	71.1	49	124.5
8	203	20.3	29	73.7	50	127.0

YARDS TO METRES

YARDS	METRES	YARDS	METRES	YARDS	METRES	YARDS	METRES	YARDS	METRES
⅛	0.11	2⅛	1.94	4⅛	3.77	6⅛	5.60	8⅛	7.43
¼	0.23	2¼	2.06	4¼	3.89	6¼	5.72	8¼	7.54
⅜	0.34	2⅜	2.17	4⅜	4.00	6⅜	5.83	8⅜	7.66
½	0.46	2½	2.29	4½	4.11	6½	5.94	8½	7.77
⅝	0.57	2⅝	2.40	4⅝	4.23	6⅝	6.06	8⅝	7.89
¾	0.69	2¾	2.51	4¾	4.34	6¾	6.17	8¾	8.00
⅞	0.80	2⅞	2.63	4⅞	4.46	6⅞	6.29	8⅞	8.12
1	0.91	3	2.74	5	4.57	7	6.40	9	8.23
1⅛	1.03	3⅛	2.86	5⅛	4.69	7⅛	6.52	9⅛	8.34
1¼	1.14	3¼	2.97	5¼	4.80	7¼	6.63	9¼	8.46
1⅜	1.26	3⅜	3.09	5⅜	4.91	7⅜	6.74	9⅜	8.57
1½	1.37	3½	3.20	5½	5.03	7½	6.86	9½	8.69
1⅝	1.49	3⅝	3.31	5⅝	5.14	7⅝	6.97	9⅝	8.80
1¾	1.60	3¾	3.43	5¾	5.26	7¾	7.09	9¾	8.92
1⅞	1.71	3⅞	3.54	5⅞	5.37	7⅞	7.20	9⅞	9.03
2	1.83	4	3.66	6	5.49	8	7.32	10	9.14

Index